Choices

Choices

A novel by
Dorothy W. Peterson

Bookcraft
Salt Lake City, Utah

To Marilyn and Mary

Library of Congress Catalog Card Number: 88–72242
ISBN 0–88494–675–4

First Printing, 1988

Printed in the United States of America

_____One

Richard Callahan sat slouched into his chair, his long, awkward legs stretched straight in front of him and crossed at the ankles. He absentmindedly ruffled his sandy blond hair as he silently questioned what he devotedly called his "purpose in life."

The stream of light coming through the library window held the evidence of a pleasant January day — not unusual for Southern California. Temperatures in the mid-seventies, the weatherman had promised — a promise someone had kept — and yet it was gloomy. *Even sunshine can cheat,* he told himself as he forced his mind back to his studies.

"Have you seen the *Times* today, Callahan?" a familiar voice intruded. At the same time the front page of the *Los Angeles Times* newspaper appeared in front of him. The January 23, 1973 date loomed at him — a date he would never forget.

Rich had seen the unbelievably small headline about halfway down the page: "Supreme Court Rule Gives Women Right to Have Abortions." He sickened at the thought of a whole society with its hands dipped in fetal blood.

He was a theology student because he wanted to serve. Life mattered and people mattered. Little unborn babies mattered. Women and their special problems mattered, too, he told himself, but this was a question of priorities — inconvenience, embarrassment, and pain balanced against human life itself. He cringed and forced his eyes away from the newsprint.

"I'm studying, Figgy." Rich didn't need to look up to know who took the two seats at his table and spread their newspaper across his books. They were both theology students like himself. The one who spoke was Larry Freundhauser. He liked to argue the significance of the fig leaf in the Creation story— especially with freshmen. Hence the nickname.

That thought made Rich's stomach turn as it brought to memory pictures of Figgy stuffing his mouth with sugary donuts and spraying crumbs across the school cafeteria table at some unsuspecting freshman while he expounded theories of sexual excesses and the resultant expulsion from Eden. It was all for shock value, of course. That wasn't Figgy's philosophy—he didn't have a philosophy unless you counted his schemes to use the church to get rich. Unfortunately, Rich knew he'd succeed. Figgy could sell a shark dentures. He'd sell his own brand of religion and make a bundle doing it. It was a shame such talent wouldn't be better used. Figgy's companion, Cal Harris, wasn't much better.

"A little grumpy today, aren't we?" Figgy leaned across the table and drummed his fingertips above the headline. Rich lifted the front page of the *Times* off his books.

"I have studying to do."

"Baker's class! I don't know why you enrolled in intercession. You deserve a month off with the rest of us."

"I don't have a rich daddy picking up the tab, remember? And I've got a family to feed. I can't afford to waste a month."

"Yeah, I heard. You and Penny can enjoy the dance without paying the piper these days. Haven't you heard of birth control?"

"Stow it, Figgy!" Rich gathered his books and papers into his sadly worn briefcase.

Figgy smiled viciously. "You know, what really surprises me, Callahan, is how you got Penny to marry you—skinny, ugly wart that you are."

Rich felt his face and neck turn red and his temples pound as he held his breath and turned to leave.

"C'mon, leave him alone. Let's go." Cal placed a plump hand on Figgy's arm. "Don't mind him." He laughed indulgently.

Figgy jerked his arm away and planted himself in front of Rich, making it difficult for him to move. "You really ought to read the paper, Callahan. I'll bet Penny's reading it right now. She'll be real interested."

Rich's jaw tightened. "You couldn't possibly know what *my* wife would be interested in," he said.

"Oh, you think not." Figgy swaggered slightly as he backed away. "She was my girl first, remember?"

"She was *never* your girl." Rich braced his right forearm against Figgy's chest and pushed past him. Cal caught Figgy in midfall and eased him to the floor. Rich sensed Figgy seething behind him as he escaped down the stairway of the large library reading room and headed for the freedom of the campus lawn and fresh air.

"You ought to read it, Dad," Figgy shouted after him, holding up the newspaper. "The court says it's not too late to get rid of that little problem of yours."

Rich stood quietly in the apartment doorway, watching beads of perspiration roll down Penny's face as she put up the last of the strips of wallpaper. Checking the clock, she reached for the smoothing brush and razor blade on the table behind her.

"Darn!" she said under her breath. "You're home early."

She turned and hurriedly straightened and smoothed the soggy paper, matching the bright flower pattern as she went. Then standing atop the step stool, she trimmed the excess paper away at the ceiling edge.

"What is this?"

"Give me a chance to explain," Penny said as she quickly stepped down to the floor and embraced him gravely, lifting her face to his.

"You can't explain this. We can't afford . . . "

"Five dollars, Rich. That's all it cost. It's even prepasted; all I needed to put it up was a package of razor blades."

"C'mon, Penny, five dollars? I know what wallpaper costs."

"Cross my heart," she insisted. "I can show you the receipt. It was the last of that money Mom sent me. We agreed I could spend it any way I chose."

He returned her embrace halfheartedly and then backed away from her.

"I was hoping you'd choose to buy food with it." He looked again at the bright pink flowers that covered their walls. "I can see why the store was trying to unload this stuff."

"I know it's bright, but that's what we need in here. The green couch and the carpet match the color of the leaves exactly, see?" With a sudden movement she pulled his head down and joined his lips to hers. He closed his eyes and enjoyed the moment, then pulled himself away.

He inspected the worn and spotted olive green carpet under his feet and the misshapen couch against the wall. "How can you say they both match the leaves when they don't match each other?"

Penny folded her hands behind her back, took a deep breath, and forced her shoulders backward. "Don't be angry. I thought you'd be pleased or I wouldn't have done all this." She sighed heavily.

Although he felt angry at first, his mood changed as he watched his wife with pleasure. He unconsciously ran his fingers over his rough face and wondered again how this "ugly wart" had managed to attract the most beautiful girl on campus. Even the paste-spattered Levi's she wore couldn't disguise her petite, shapely form. Her large blue eyes dominated her pretty face. Her blond hair haloed her fair skin with a profusion of softness.

Rich knew he'd stared too long when Penny ducked away from him to look in the entry mirror. She frowned at herself, loosened a barrette that had slipped from its place, smoothed back her curls, and refastened the clip across them.

He smiled. "What can I say?" he began, his tired mind racing to find something positive. "You've done a nice job." In two giant steps he crossed the room that served as living room and dining area and unloaded his books onto the dinette table. "Now you get to work all evening, come home in time to fall into bed, wake up in a few hours sick, throw up all morning while I attend classes, spend tomorrow afternoon cleaning house and doing laundry you should have done today, and then go back to work again."

"I can handle it," she said gaily.

"I just think . . . " He slumped into a rusty folding chair nearby and stared again at the shapely body that housed their unborn child, and he wondered how long it would be before her condition was obvious. He rarely looked at her these days without feeling pain over their decision to accept children whenever the Lord saw fit to send them. It was unwise, he thought again as he pondered the problems that that decision had caused. Yet there were other feelings — feelings of pride and anticipation, feelings that were stronger than their negative counterparts. *Penny's happy and excited. I should be too,* he told himself when his fears overcame him. *It'll all work out.*

"I just think," he began again, "that if you want things like wallpaper, you ought to let me do it."

"Oh, terrific. You work as many hours as I do and have a full class load to boot. Your doing even more makes a lot of sense."

"I can handle it." He mimicked her delighted confidence.

"So can I."

He smiled. "Yeah, I guess you can."

He rubbed the tension from his face and stretched halfheartedly. "Have you seen the paper today?"

"Yes."

"What'd you think?"

"It's what you expected."

"Yeah, but I'd hoped . . . "

"I know." She leaned over and kissed him again.

He relished the kiss and responded willingly this time.

When she returned to her work he asked, "Are you about finished?"

"Just need to clean up this mess."

"Then let me help."

"Don't you have studying to do?" she asked as he took a pail of scummy water out of her hands.

"Don't you have dinner to fix?"

"Touché," she said.

He picked up the damp newspapers that protected the floor and carpet and stuffed them into a wastebasket, while she washed her hands and then began making hamburger patties for their evening meal.

"Figgy caught me in the library today," Rich said.

"Oh, great! What'd he want?"

"He's heard the campus gossip about us."

"It's not gossip."

"Sorry, poor choice of words. Anyway, he had to get his digs in. He had the *Times* and suggested the court decision might benefit us."

Rich continued to work in silence until he became aware of Penny standing at the kitchen's edge. She leaned against the narrow partition that separated the kitchen from the living room.

All the windows across the front of the tiny apartment were open wide. Rich felt a cooling breeze drift past him. It was dusk, and the warmer temperatures of the day were giving way to a cool January night. He closed the window nearest him and looked back at his wife. She was mindlessly molding a piece of ground meat, and she had tears in her eyes.

"You're not thinking he's right, are you?" she asked.

"No, of course not."

"Rich?"

"It's going to be rough, Pen."

"I know, but we'll make it."

"We're just making it now. I have a year and a half more of graduate school and work on my thesis, and you'll only be able to work another six months— tops." She had been shutting out the fact that having this baby was not all joy and happiness. It was time she faced it. Rich shivered again and reached for the last of the open windows.

"What are you getting at? You think this was all a mistake?" Penny dropped the hamburger into the hot frying pan on the stove. It sizzled and popped furiously. She grabbed another wad of meat and began slapping at it. "Maybe the marriage was a mistake, too." She turned her back toward him.

"No. Honey, c'mon. You know better than that."

Rich pushed the last of the trash into the wastebasket near the sink, picked up a bar of soap, and scrubbed the newsprint from his hands and arms. Then he turned to his wife, tightened both arms around her waist, and snuggled close to her. She leaned back against him. He liked the feeling that he could take care of her and their child. If only it were as easy as strong arms held firmly in place.

"You know I love you, don't you?" he said.

"Yes."

He backed away from her. "You want salad tonight?" he asked.

"I guess so." She glanced over her shoulder to see him searching through the fridge. "Bottom drawer . . . see?"

He took out what he wanted and began breaking the lettuce into a large bowl.

Penny turned the hamburgers, then looked back to see how her not-too-adept kitchen helper was doing. "Did you get the tomatoes for that?" she asked.

"I didn't see any," he replied, his voice breaking in the middle.

Penny moved toward the fridge, taking a sidelong look at Rich. "I know there are some in here. Let me look," she said, and opened the fridge door. "Here they are. They've been washed, so . . . " She handed him the fresh fruit. "It's the court decision, isn't it? You're more upset than I thought."

"Have you read the article?"

"Not really—just a couple of paragraphs."

"I have. I've studied it until I have it practically memorized. You know, Penny, it's incredible to me that this could happen. The majority opinion doesn't even recognize the child's existence until after the sixth month of pregnancy. The Supreme Court makes a point of the new procedures being *safe*. I read it over five times trying to decide what was strange about that statement. I finally figured it out. It doesn't say it's safe for the mother. That's what it means, of course, but the value of the other life is so insignificant that the justices don't even bother to clarify the statement."

Penny wrapped protective arms around her body and leaned back against the edge of the stove.

Her sudden movement drew Rich's attention. She looked shockingly pale and weak. "Are you all right?" he asked.

"Yes. I just feel a little sick."

Rich took Penny in his arms and held her. "So do I," he said. "So do I."

Two

"Cybil, I told you to change your school clothes before you do that!" cried Marianne Renwick to her ten-year-old daughter. The slender, freckled child sat cross-legged on the garage floor with her skirt stretched tightly across her lap. On top of the skirt three tiny kittens squirmed and mewed in sightless frenzy, searching for nourishment. Cybil cradled the fourth kitten in her left hand and held a doll-sized nursing bottle to its eager mouth. The child's dress was filthy.

"But they're hungry now. I couldn't wait to feed them."

"I fed them myself an hour ago. They'd wait another ten minutes while you changed." The mother shook her head and sighed.

Mrs. Renwick eased herself onto the floor next to her little girl. May in Nebraska was still cold, though not freezing, and the cement floor chilled her denim-covered legs. She looked at her daughter and wondered how she stood the cold with only a thin cotton skirt to protect her. A scolding was in order, she supposed, but she bit her tongue instead and turned her attention back to the kittens. She filled another bottle with the formula the veterinarian had given them, and picked up the smallest of the kittens from Cybil's lap. The little kitten licked aimlessly at the nipple, then finally took hold of it and sucked.

Cybil touched the kitten to her cheek, closing her eyes as she relished the feeling. "I think Sassy's mean not to feed her own babies. What if I didn't feed _her_ for a while?" Her mouth turned down in a pout.

Marianne let her hand drop to her lap as she stared at her daughter. _"Who_ feeds her?"

"Well, I do . . . sometimes."

"That's more like it." The mother turned her attention back to the kitten. "Animals are like humans in some ways. Starving Sassy won't change that. C'mon, little one," Marianne pleaded with the kitten in her hand. "You have to eat." She struggled another couple of minutes to keep the sleepy kitten awake long enough to finish the bottle. Finally giving up, she put the creature in the cushioned basket beside the water heater. "I'm afraid this one isn't going to make it. It's a shame."

"They're not going to die! I won't let them!" Cybil insisted as she picked up another from her lap.

"I don't want them to die, either, but you've got to face that possibility."

Cybil felt the cold, wet snout of her dog against the back of her neck. "Teddy, don't!" she squealed.

The dog relaxed onto the garage floor next to his mistress, his head resting across her left leg. He sniffed curiously at the kittens in Cybil's lap.

"Aren't they cute?" the girl said.

Teddy barked loudly and backed suddenly away from her. Continuing to bark, he lunged back and forth, toward the kittens and then away again.

"Teddy!" Cybil objected. "Mom, get him away. He's frightening them."

"He won't hurt them."

"He might," Cybil whined again.

"All right, I'll lock him outside," Mrs. Renwick said as she took hold of the dog's collar. "C'mon, Teddy, outside with you."

Mrs. Renwick looked again at her daughter's soiled dress. "Be sure you put that dress in the laundry basket when you take it off, and tomorrow change your school clothes before you come out here."

"Sure, Mom."

Mrs. Renwick shook her head as she left the garage with Teddy in tow.

Cybil stood outside the back screen door, hearing her parents talking. Their muffled voices reached her ears and she waited on the steps, catching the drops from a light spring shower on her tongue. The raindrops, clustered in the elm trees, sparkled like diamonds as the sun broke through. Life was simple and good. How could kittens die in a simply wonderful world like this one? She watched her father set his portfolio on the dining room table on his way into the kitchen from the front door.

"Ralph? That you?" Her mother looked through the kitchen door when she heard the front door open. "More work tonight?" she asked.

"We've got a meeting with Mr. Kemp tomorrow. I've got to get these drawings done."

"I'd sure like to know what Peter's definition of partnership is," Marianne said half under her breath as she turned back to her work.

"Don't start on me, Marianne." He followed his wife into the kitchen.

"I mean it, Ralph. You do all the work."

"You don't see what he does. Besides, you have no reason to complain. The company's been good to us. How else could I spoil my two favorite girls like I do?" He put a slender arm around his wife's shoulder and pulled her into him, kissing her forehead at the same time.

"I don't know about me, but spoiled is right if you're talking about Cybil."

Ralph sighed. "I don't need more problems tonight, Marianne."

"You never want to hear about problems with Cybil, but we've got—"

"What's she done now?"

"She just ignores everything I tell her."

"That's not my fault . . . oh, hi, Punkin," her father said, winking, as Cybil opened the back door. "How are the kittens?"

"Fine. Mama says the little one isn't going to make it."

He looked scornfully at his wife. "As wonderful as Mama is, she doesn't know everything. C'mon, baby, give your dad a big hug." Ralph bent his tall slender frame down to greet his little girl.

Cybil's pout turned into smiles and she wrapped eager arms around her daddy's neck. "They won't die, will they, Daddy?"

"Not if you work hard at keeping them alive."

"She—work hard? She's in school most of the day," Marianne interjected. "I'm the one who—"

Ralph turned abruptly toward her. "You want to take them to the pound?" he asked, anger building in his voice.

"No, no! You can't let her do that!" Cybil screamed at her father.

Marianne looked at her whimpering child and then at her husband. "I don't want to watch them starve to death," she finally said.

"You won't have to. Cybil will see to that, won't you, Punkin?"

A smile had returned to Cybil's face. "What a nice daddy you are. You are so nice to me. I love you, Daddy." She tugged at her daddy's hand. "Come and see the kittens," she pleaded. "They'll have their eyes open soon."

She smiled sweetly at him, knowing he'd do anything at all for her for a smile and a hug. An old softie, that's what he was. Yes, the world was simple and wonderful.

_____ Three

Jeff stood quietly with Maggie close beside him, their fingers tightly intertwined. He turned to look at his bride and found her gazing up at him. He openly returned her gaze. She looked more beautiful than he'd ever remembered seeing her. She was dressed in white, her lovely face and dark hair beautiful against the softness of her white veil.

Maggie blushed and leaned into his embrace. "I guess I'd better stop staring. Someone might get the wrong idea," she said as she pressed her cheek against his shoulder. "Sorry if I can't take my eyes off you."

Jeff smiled. Maggie's look delighted him as it always did. He released her hand, put his arm around her waist, and drew her to him. He smiled self-consciously as he looked around the room and wondered if anyone was watching them. That thought made him laugh. *Here we are in the sealing room of the Oakland Temple at our wedding*, he mused. Their guests filed silently into the splendid chamber, and they all watched them. After all, Jeff and Maggie were the main attraction at this event. He didn't care; let them watch.

The sealing room was luminous with light from the crystal chandelier that hung above the altar. A softer, warmer light filtered in through the window. The altar was upholstered in white brocade and was loosely draped with a white hand-crocheted coverlet. Large full-length mirrors faced each other from both ends of the room. The effect was a never-ending replication of all who attended there. Jeff felt the warmth of the room and reflected on how happy he was.

The bridal couple was directed to sit in chairs with their backs to one of the mirrors and opposite the podium where the temple president would officiate. When everyone else was seated they took their seats.

Jeff looked around the room for his sister, the only family member who had investigated and joined the Church with him. He winked at her as their eyes met across the room. The rest of the people were Maggie's family and friends, many of whom were unfamiliar to him.

He took Maggie's hand and squeezed it. What a blessing she was to him. His mind captured and released memory after memory of their courtship . . .

She had been seated at the breakfast bar in Joanne's apartment, her long, shapely legs barely touching the floor. She was dressed comfortably in medium length shorts and a T-shirt, her dark, curly hair tied up in a colorful scarf. Her fair skin beautifully set off her large, dark eyes.

She smiled warmly but didn't look directly at him.

Shy, he noted. *But that's okay. I like shy girls. I'll make a point of our becoming friends.*

That was the plan.

Jeff laughed silently — a laugh no one else in the room noticed except Maggie, who was sitting so close to him that she was surely aware of his every breath.

She shifted her veil so it would not obscure her view of him and whispered, "Something funny?"

"I was just remembering," he whispered back.

12

Maggie had had an old Volkswagen that she had nursed along through the last couple of years of college and the two years since graduation. She was determined to make the old heap last until she had enough money to buy a newer one without having to go into debt. One afternoon he came by to find Maggie half buried under the hood of her old car, her face smeared with grease and oil. She had a library auto-repair manual open on the fender with a piece of plastic wrap draped across to protect it; she had a wrench in hand and was attempting to remove the car's generator. (That would prove to be an unforgettable picture.)

"What on earth are you doing?" he asked as he approached her.

She cringed as her grease-smeared face peeked around the edge of the open hood and then disappeared again inside the engine well. "I'm fixing my car," she said without looking at him again.

"Are you serious?" He intruded his head and upper body under the hood.

"This isn't so hard. If that kid at the garage can do this, I'm sure I can. He was going to charge me more than a hundred bucks for a simple repair," she muttered as she returned to her work.

Jeff laughed silently as he watched her. Her face and hands were filthy, and her clothing hadn't fared much better. Her naturally curly mop of hair, which she normally kept in strict control, bushed in every direction. He laughed again as he tried to remember ever seeing any of the other girls he'd dated looking this bad. He knew for sure none of them would have attempted to fix her own car. The smell of the dirt and grease penetrated his senses and brought memories of the sweet perfume she'd worn on their last date together.

"Haven't you ever fixed anything on your car?" she asked.

"Sure, but I'm a guy . . . " He stopped short. She frowned. He knew he'd said the wrong thing, but there was no way out of it.

That moment was the first hint of real feeling he had for her. From then on he pursued her, sometimes relentlessly. Other times, when he felt her resistance, he eased off for a while.

Then came the time when he felt so in love with her that he tried to pressure her into physical intimacy. There had been some discussion early in their relationship about her strange religion and the standards of morality it embraced. He had no interest in the doctrines of her church, so Maggie had long since stopped talking to him about them. But he had understood her moral stand and had kept his distance as he had promised. Over the months though, their feelings for each other had grown until, for his part, he felt he could no longer contain them. Surely, he reasoned, the moral question was a moot one by now.

He'd prepared dinner for her, and later, when he made his suggestion, they were watching the ocean through the picture window of his beachside condo. "I can't," she said . . .

He backed away from her, walked to the window, and looked out. "Why?" he whispered, as if he didn't really want her to hear it. Then he turned toward her and said it again more deliberately. "Why?"

She didn't answer.

"My—" he started, then he stopped himself as he saw her wince. *Reverence for the Lord's name,* he thought. *Another vestige of her outworn religion . . . I ought to walk away from this while I still can.* He laughed silently and turned away. Walk away from it! If only he could! He ran tense hands back through his hair and grasped the crown of his head. He cursed under his breath as he felt anger building. He dropped his hands to his sides and wheeled back around to face her.

"We're both adults, for . . . heaven's sake! We're not kids! And this is the eighties, not the fifties."

"I believe it's wrong to have sexual intercourse outside the marriage covenant," she said deliberately. "You know that." Tears filled her eyes, and she let them spill onto her cheeks unashamedly. "The fact that it's the eighties doesn't change that for me."

"I love you," he said. Her perfume filled his nostrils and his head reeled with thoughts of her. His stereo played soft music barely loud enough to hear. The melody, mingled with the muted sound of the ocean's roll, created a mood that was irresistible. "We love each other," he added.

"I know," she responded.

"Isn't that enough? Enough! Maggie, that's all there is!"

"No! No, Jeff, there's more — there's much, much more. Love is the beginning — and the end, too — but there's an eternity in between, and I want it all."

Jeff looked at her closely. Her eyes pleaded with him to understand. His thoughts whirred past him like the reel of a giant recording machine. When the machine stopped, it revealed a vague memory. He'd all but forgotten — no, he'd been a part of the world for so long that he'd dismissed it as a myth. " 'Who can find a virtuous woman?' " he whispered to himself as he slowly turned back toward the window.

"What?" Maggie asked.

He turned half around so she could hear and, taking care not to catch her eye, he answered, " 'Who can find a virtuous woman? for her price is far above rubies.' It's a passage from the Bible — Proverbs, I think. My mother used to quote it to my sisters every time they left the house with a boyfriend. With six sisters, that was a lot of dates. I guess I've heard it a thousand times. It was a long time ago. I'd forgotten."

He knew now how much she'd loved him then. It had taken real faith and determination to say no to him, and he loved her all the more for it. It was then, or soon after that, he had decided to marry her. He remembered his shock when she turned him down. They'd driven up the coast to find privacy from neighbors and had begun to walk along the beach . . .

"I can't marry you," she repeated.

"Why?" This was incredible. He had lacked confidence as he posed the question, but he'd never doubted what the answer would be.

"You won't understand." She slumped down and sat cross-legged on the sand.

The air was cool and damp. The beach was empty except for a flock of seagulls feeding nearby. Maggie shivered and drew her knees up to her body and wrapped sweatered arms around them.

Jeff walked out to the water's edge looking out to sea. The dank smell of saltwater hung heavy in the air. He watched a small vessel beyond them careen and dip in the rough ocean. The same waves that jostled the tiny craft crashed over the rocks a few yards away, then lapped at his feet like a whimpering puppy begging for a bone. He continued to watch as the foamy water ebbed away, revealing tiny crevices in the sand.

"When I marry, it must be to someone of my own faith," she said.

He turned and looked at her thoughtfully for a moment, then took a few steps and crouched down in front of her. Sitting on his heels, he forced her to look at him. "You're right"—he nearly shouted to be heard over the screeching of the birds and the roar of the sea—"I don't understand."

"It's really important to me to marry a member of my church."

She went on to explain what was truly unfathomable to him. He didn't understand, but he was forced to accept it. He left the beachside condo to move back to New York where his family lived, and she stayed on without him. The only thing that kept him from hating her for the hurt she'd caused him was the sure knowledge that she was just as miserable as he.

It wasn't long after that that he had a visitor.

"Jeff," the stage manager called as Jeff finished rehearsing a scene with the leading lady's stand-in. "You'll do fine," he told her before he stepped off the stage and moved up the aisle toward the back of the theater.

He picked up a small towel from the back of a front-row seat and wiped perspiration off his face and neck. "You wanted me, Gene?" he asked, straining to see where the voice had come from. Quickly his eyes adjusted to the dim light after the bright lights of the stage, and he saw a woman standing next to Gene at the back of the theater.

"You have company," Gene answered.

"Whew, it's hot in here, isn't it?" He wiped his face a second time before greeting his visitor.

Just then they heard the whir of the fans as the air conditioning came on. "Not for long, though," he added.

"They cool it for the audience but not for the actors," the woman said with a smile.

"That's about right. Actors are used to the heat of the bright lights. It wouldn't seem natural to them if rehearsals were cool. Let's go into the lobby. It'll be nicer there."

"I won't keep you wondering," the lady began as soon as she was seated. "I'm Gretchen, Maggie Barnett's sister."

"Gretchen," he repeated, as he relaxed and leaned back against the wall and away from her. He felt a pang of hurt pull at him. "Uh, what do I say? Hello."

"I know this is awkward. It is for me, too. I really debated before I decided to find you. I'm in town visiting friends and I . . . well, I've been here a week already. We go home tomorrow . . . " She stood and walked away from him. "I . . . don't know why I came."

Jeff laughed. "Curiosity, maybe."

"Oh, no, really."

"It's okay, I'm not offended. Listen, maybe this would be easier over a meal. There's a little café around the corner; I'll buy you a sandwich."

"Oh, no, I couldn't let you do that."

"I insist. I wish I had time for a nicer place, but I've got to be back here in an hour."

"A sandwich is fine, thanks."

The café had become a favorite place of Jeff's. It was exactly what he would expect a New York haunt, just around the corner from an off-Broadway theater, to look like. It was dimly lit, with a bar along one long wall. The atmosphere was old and musty and heavy with the smell of liquor and tobacco smoke. It was nearly empty in the late afternoon, but it would be packed solid with the theater crowd when the play was over.

"I am curious about one thing, Jeff," Gretchen began once they were seated and the waitress had taken their order. "Had you taken this part in the play before you left L.A.?"

Jeff put his water glass down and sat back in his seat. *What's she after?* he asked himself as he examined her more closely. She was prettier than Maggie, if that were possible, although not as tall and shapely. Her manner was more self-assured and commanding. Maggie had said that Gretchen liked to take charge of things. He could believe it. Jeff watched his fingers as he turned the pedestalled water glass. "You mean before I asked Maggie to marry me?"

"Whatever."

He thought carefully before he answered. "No," he said.

Gretchen frowned, and Jeff wondered what she was thinking.

"Are you good in it?" she asked.

Jeff laughed. "Maggie said you were direct."

"I'm sorry. I only meant—"

"No, that's okay. I think I know what you meant. The play didn't get rave reviews at first, but it's a hit just the same. That sometimes happens if the promoters do a good job before it opens, and sell lots of tickets. People come to see it in spite of the critics and decide for themselves. If they like it the word gets around."

"The public likes it, then."

"Yes. The critics have taken a second look. I've been mentioned favorably in late reviews. I guess I do my share."

"Are you a major character?"

"Supporting role."

"I'm impressed, I must say."

"Then I pass inspection?"

Gretchen frowned again.

"Can I get you anything else?" the waitress asked as she put their sandwiches and drinks in front of them.

Jeff waited while Gretchen shook her head, then he said, "No, thank you."

"I'm sorry, Jeff. I'm afraid you misunderstand me. I'm not here to *appraise* you. Maggie's been upset since you left. To be absolutely honest, the rest of the family has felt quite relieved. A sparsely employed actor/musician is not what good old Mom and Dad had in mind for their daughter."

Ouch! Jeff thought without showing it. He waited for a moment, then spoke. "I haven't been out of work since I was fifteen years old. Did Maggie tell you I also teach school?"

"Yes, of course, I only meant . . . oh, dear, I guess I've done it again. I'm sorry."

"I have degrees in music and drama; I'm well prepared for what I do, and I'm good at it. I'm fully employed now, and when I'm not, I teach at the college level. I don't consider that unstable. In L.A. I was a member of a rock group that has done pretty well for itself. We worked steadily in clubs around the area."

"Maggie told me that. That's part of what I don't understand. You gave that up to come here with no job waiting for you."

"My agent had arranged an audition for this play."

"A mere chance at a play that may or may not have even opened—that doesn't make sense."

"That's what this business is all about." Jeff continued the conversation only half-conscious of what was being said. His thoughts turned back to those few days it had taken him to get his life turned around so he could leave California. They were painful days, and he frowned at their memory.

"No. I'm sorry," Gretchen continued. "I'm too practical to accept that. Frankly, Jeff, it demonstrates a certain instability. My sister deserves a better life than that promises . . . "

She stopped talking and Jeff became aware that she was watching him. He forced a smile and pushed his plate away. "I've got to get back to the theater," he said as he pulled a large bill from his pocket and left it on the table. "Can I get you a taxi?" he asked as he stood and turned toward the exit.

"Jeff, wait." Gretchen slid out from behind the table and bounded after him. She grabbed his elbow before he reached the door. "It was Maggie, wasn't it? She drove you away when she turned you down. The family had never considered that, and apparently Maggie hadn't, either. She told us you had a job offer in New York and had left. Well, you can see how that looked to us—flighty, disinterested."

Jeff struggled to control his anger. *The family!* he thought. *What business was it of theirs?* He couldn't look at Maggie's oldest sister and he continued to try to pull away from her. "Listen, I don't want to be rude, but I do have to go."

"You said an hour; it's only been forty minutes. Please, can we talk?"

Gretchen had a change of heart about Jeff before she left the café that day, or so Jeff hoped. In fact, it was the first real hope he'd had concerning his and Maggie's relationship. Hope for something good in life was the magical essence that made life worth living, and yet that same hope often caused pain. He wondered if he'd ever get any feedback from Gretchen's visit. He hoped that Maggie would contact him. He gave it a few days, then began looking for a letter. Every time the phone rang, he jumped to answer it. A month passed before he finally gave up on that idea. Then the day after Christmas a call did come . . .

"Hello, Jeff, this is Gretchen. Remember me? I'm Maggie Barnett's sister."

"Yes." Jeff felt his throat constrict.

"This is crazy, I know . . . I, ah . . . "

Jeff took advantage of the pause to ask, "How is Maggie?"

"Oh, she's fine. She's enjoying Christmas break from school—glad to be home, with the family, I mean. She's been kind of lonely."

Jeff didn't respond.

"Well, anyway. I guess I'd better get to the point. I was wondering if you could fly out here for a couple of days. Maggie would love it, and the family would like to meet you."

"I don't know, Gretchen. I don't see any point in it . . . "

"That's just what I'm telling you, there is a point to it."

The ache in Jeff's middle that had begun the moment Gretchen identified herself changed, and he felt adrenaline surge through his body. He sat down and leaned back in his chair, then leaned forward nervously.

"Does Maggie know about this?" Jeff finally asked.

"No."

"Because she'd say no if you asked her."

There was a pause.

"People often don't know what's best for them," Gretchen finally answered.

"And you do." Jeff felt deflated and sank back into his chair.

"I think so: I've known Maggie a lot longer than you have."

"There's been so much hurt over this already, it just seems to me it'd be better to let it alone."

"I can't guarantee anything, Jeff. But things have changed at this end. I think you'll be glad—you'll both be glad—if you come."

There was another pause.

"I'd like to come, but I'd prefer it if Maggie knew about it and agreed."

Gretchen was very pushy; she'd finally convinced him to come without Maggie's consent. Sitting next to his bride in the temple, he was glad she had. Those were the most eventful two days of his life, until now.

His memory clicked off pictures of those two days as fast as his mind could assimilate them. There were their private walks, rare moments alone together when they felt close again after their painful separation. There was the family picnic, with the three-legged race they won; that was an event. There was the talent show; he and Maggie sang together. And the evening out with her brothers and sisters. The few moments they spent together after that evening out was the turning point in their relationship. They talked in the entry for a few minutes with her brothers and sisters and their spouses until the others excused themselves and went to bed. Then, taking Jeff's hand, Maggie led him into the kitchen.

Still clinging to Maggie's right hand, Jeff grabbed a nearby kitchen stool, pulled it under him, and turned her around to face him all in the same motion. He clasped his hands behind her back at the waist and urged her closer. With playful reluctance she complied and laid her forearms gently across his shoulders and chest.

"It was a nice evening," he began. She agreed. After more small talk and a long awkward pause, Jeff went on, "I, uh . . . don't see how we can go on like this, do you?"

"No."

"No?" He was encouraged but disappointed in her answer. "Can't you say more than that?"

She looked past him and stared blankly.

"What can we do about it?" he asked.

She didn't answer, and the resulting silence pained him. He was about to speak again when Maggie touched his lips gently with her fingertips and began her belated response.

"I'm sorry," she said, clenching her lips between her teeth and looking away momentarily. Looking back at him, she began again. "Nothing's changed, Jeff." She reached across his shoulder for a napkin from the holder tucked against the back wall of the kitchen counter. After having wiped away her tears, she looked at him again.

Her face contorted with pain. He ached for her and wished he could take the hurt away. In a burst of emotion, she thrust her arms tightly around his neck and, pressing her wet face into his shoulder, she wept uncontrollably.

Her sudden embrace caught Jeff by surprise, and he sat there stunned, but only briefly. Then he responded with strong arms stretched snugly around her back and a kiss pressed firmly against the nape of her neck. When he finally relaxed his hold, Maggie backed away, wiped her face again, turned toward the back windows, and stood in silence.

The long silence gave Jeff time to think and understand better than he had before. This religion of Maggie's — this obsession she had for a dream that he'd seen as ethereal foolishness — would not be displaced by anything, including a love so strong that it tore at her. He'd known it was important to her, but he was beginning to see that he had not understood just how dearly her dream was held.

Having spent the past two days with her and her family had helped him to understand better what she'd tried to explain to him on the beach. Her family wasn't so different from his own, and yet they had something . . .

"You're right, Jeff. We can't go on like this," she said, interrupting his reverie.

There were no lights on. Moonlight filtered in through the window behind Maggie. Her features were illuminated as the moon's glow caressed her shoulder and caught the highlights of her profile. To anyone else the image would have been spectre-like, but to Jeff, it was beautiful. She had stopped crying, and as she stood there, she took on the appearance of someone whose courage had been challenged to the extreme, and who would quickly end the foray before her strength waned altogether. She was about to speak, but she stopped abruptly; then, with a new issue of tears and an apparent change of mind, she cried out, "No, no, I can't." She turned away from him again, this time with arms crossed at her waist and fists clenched tightly to elbows as if she were in great pain. Jeff ached for her.

Finally she turned back and, wiping her tears away, she continued. "Don't force me to turn you down again." Without a breath in between, she sped through protracted confessions of love, devotion, desire — feelings she had never fully expressed to him before. When she was finished, she sank exhausted onto a stool at the end of the counter, and, staring mindlessly at her hands in her lap, she went on, this time expressing things Jeff had himself felt many times before. "The way we feel about each other can't be wrong, but I know that what I want for myself is right, too . . . " She laughed hopelessly and said, "I guess I want to have my cake and eat it too—but what's wrong with that?" She looked at him as if she thought he could supply the answer. "I know one thing for sure—something my parents are very wrong about—I will never get over you." She was looking intently at him now, her eyes still laden with tears.

"Why can't this just be simple—the way I've always planned? You know, when I first decided that I was going to be a teacher it was all so simple. There was a certain order of things to be done, and I did them—high school, then college, teaching credentials, job applications, decisions about where I wanted to teach. Even when my best friend and I decided we wanted to work at the same school—do you know the chances of our finding that?—we never doubted it could be done. We just applied together everywhere, and when the offers came at the same time from not only the same district but the same school, we accepted them as if it were our right. It was all so easy." She looked down and asked again in a whisper, "Why can't this be that simple?"

That night, for the first time he had begun to understand how important her desire was for what she considered a proper marriage. He had gone back to New York with little resolved, except that he had privately determined that he would look into her church. Nothing to lose and a whole lot to gain—that had been his attitude. He fought a desire at first to join the Church no matter what. He knew that that wouldn't make either of them happy. Soon it became apparent that he needn't worry about that.

As soon as he arrived home in New York he contacted the Church mission headquarters and began the missionary lessons. It was hard for him at first because much of what they taught him was so foreign to what he'd been taught as a child. And yet there were important similarities. His parents were devoted Catholics, and he'd been reared in their church. He'd always been impressed with the great faith they seemed to possess but had never acquired it for himself. His mother had taught him to pray. He loved his mother and respected her devotion to her God. The things she taught him lingered in him and yet did not possess him as they did her.

Then one day he was reading the Book of Mormon and began reading from the little book of Enos.

"Behold, I went to hunt beasts in the forests; and the words which I had often heard my father speak concerning eternal life, and the joy of the saints, sunk deep into my heart. And my soul hungered; and I kneeled down before my Maker, and I cried unto him in mighty prayer and supplication for mine own soul; and all the day long did I cry unto him; yea, and when the night came I did still raise my voice high that it reached the heavens. And there came a voice unto me, saying: Enos, thy sins are forgiven thee, and thou shalt be blessed. And I, Enos, knew that God could not lie; wherefore, my guilt was swept away."

Jeff felt a warm sensation rise along his backbone until it made his neck and face flush. The blood vessels deep within his head seemed to dilate and cause the blood to flow more freely. He felt light-headed but not faint. He sat up straighter in his chair and read the passage again. He had seen his mother pray like that — for those she loved. He was certain she had prayed for him. He read again, and key phrases took hold of his soul. "The words which I had often heard my father speak . . . sunk deep into my heart. And my soul hungered. . . . And I . . . knew that God could not lie." It seemed as if it had been included in the book just for him.

The missionaries had marked a passage at the end of the book that promised that the Holy Ghost would bear witness of the truth in the book if the reader would but ask. He had prayed about it — sincerely. This was his answer and he knew it. Jeff, too, "knew that God could not lie." He carefully marked his place and closed the book. It was not the end of his reading. He would finish the book, and somehow he knew he would have many more experiences like this one. But for now this was enough. He would ponder what he'd learned before he went on.

He was committed, and it had nothing to do with his feelings for Maggie. He was grateful for that. He embraced her religion with enthusiasm.

And that was what had brought him with her to the temple.

"Maggie, you're a beautiful bride." Jeff took her hand in his. Maggie smiled, blushed a little, and replied, "Thank you."

The temple president, a plump, gray-haired man, arrived, shuffled through his scriptures, then folded his hands across the open pages before he spoke.

"You know, I like to see couples here holding hands as you are now. Look around the room at your friends and family."

Jeff and Maggie complied.

"Those couples who are sitting next to each other are holding hands. Isn't that interesting? The temple service does that every time." He looked back at the bridal couple and continued. "I hope you'll remember that, and not just when you come to the temple."

Jeff squeezed Maggie's hand and smiled broadly. She pressed her cheek against his shoulder.

"I can see that you will," the president said, nodding. "Jeff, you don't look as nervous now as you did earlier today."

Jeff laughed pleasantly and answered, "No, sir."

"You've got a beautiful young woman there. Do you know it?"

"Yes, I do." He squeezed Maggie's hand again, but didn't look at her.

"She's a worthy companion. Well, I'm sure you're anxious to make her yours forever, so let's continue . . . "

The next few words were lost to Jeff. "Yours forever" echoed in his mind. He took her arm and wrapped it under his and pulled her closer to him. "Yours forever." He blinked a tear away.

_____Four

Rich watched Penny for a minute as they drove into Chamberlain, Nebraska, a small midwestern college town. It was January, and snow covered roofs and lawns and sparkled in the sun. Streets and walks were clear, and a steady stream of water ran down drainage ditches. Curbs lined the streets in the middle of town where Founder's Square and the city offices stood. Main Street reminded Rich of Main Street, USA in Disneyland, complete with Willard's Emporium. The shops even sported false facades like the ones they'd seen in western movies. They were, however, well kept and attractive. The streets on the town's outskirts were curbless. Mud puddled in the roadside ditches. Penny was effervescent as she looked first this way, then that, trying to catch every detail of their new home.

A parish in a small midwestern town was a dream come true for Rich and Penny. It had been more than ten years since he had finished his schooling, and they were finally where they wanted to be. He sighed happily and mentally pinched himself as he watched his wife's awe-filled face. He wondered if he should awaken the children, who were all napping in the back of the family van. The only snow they'd ever seen was on their annual one-day excursions to Arrowhead. He knew they associated it exclusively with pine trees and Santa Claus. *But no*, he thought, *let them sleep. We'll settle in the new house first and then spend the day tomorrow exploring Chamberlain.*

"This is bigger than I'd imagined from your description," Penny said.

"Really? I guess I exaggerated the town's smallness. Compared to what southern Californians call small town, this is *really* small town."

"It's charming," Penny responded.

He turned right at Chapel Drive. The block-long avenue ended at the front steps of the church Rich was to administer. The large white wood structure filled the immediate expanse of the horizon. It made an impressive picture viewed from the van's front window.

"Oh!" Penny exclaimed. "It's as beautiful as you described. How old did you say it was?"

"The original church was built in 1893, so it'll be a century in another eight years. It's expanded since then, of course. The old chapel faces the other direction around the corner. It's the children's Sunday School now. Would you like to drive around it?"

"Yes, please!"

The church and its auxiliary buildings and grounds occupied a full city block. The old two-story house that had been the home of the church's minister had been converted into a parochial school serving preschool through second-grade children. As they drove by, they heard the school bell ring, and a few seconds later the doors flew open and released a horde of red-cheeked children to the playground outside.

"That's where Timothy and Rachel will go to school," Rich said. "Caroline and Bobby will go to the public school around the next corner." He pointed the way as he turned around the last side of the block.

"Our house is just a block away?"

"Yes. It's this way." He turned right at the next corner and headed down State Street away from the church square. Rich felt his heart race as they neared their new home. He'd visited Chamberlain two months ago when he'd first received the appointment to the town's nondenominational community church. He'd found the house and had put everything they had in savings as a deposit on it. He had been sure Penny would like it. It had seemed perfect then. Now he was nervous as he thought of his beloved wife seeing it for the first time. He pulled a handkerchief from his pocket and wiped perspiration from his upper lip.

"It's on the corner a couple of blocks further," he said as he turned left. "It has a wonderful fenced yard and lots of room." Look — it's the big gold one at the end of the next block."

As he neared the house, a small group of boisterous people claimed his attention. They had gathered in front of a large flat-roofed building a block or two from his new home. He slowed as he passed by. Half a dozen men and women carried signs and chanted monotonously. They'd confronted a couple who'd just emerged from a car at the curb. The man pushed his way through the group and shouted obscenities above the din of their chant. Rich could see neighbors on both sides peering out their windows, some venturing out to their front porches.

Penny hopped out of the car the moment it stopped in their driveway and perused every inch of the house's exterior. Rich stood pondering what he'd seen and what it might have meant.

Penny took his hand and pulled at him to join her. She had seen the disturbance, too, but she was more interested in her new home.

Rich pried his eyes away from the scene down the street and enjoyed Penny's exuberance. The house was a two–story wood structure with ornate trim along the eaves and around the porch railing. The porch reached three quarters of the way around the house and was completely covered by the extended roof. The color was not a garish gold as Rich had remembered it. It was more of a warm ecru. White trim edged every detail. A porch swing hung from a crossbeam above, and two wicker chairs sat on either side of the swing.

The children had awakened as the van stopped, and they now ran happily through the snow.

"Come on, kids," Penny said. "Let's go in and look around."

Rich pulled the keys from his pocket and unlocked the front door. The children ran in first, then Penny took a deep breath and stepped across the threshold. Rich watched only her.

"Oh!" she said again. "It's beautiful."

Rich followed her from the entry hall through an ornate archway into the living room. He watched and tried to see the room through her eyes. She seemed pleased, but that was like her. It was unexpectedly warm. Sunlight filled the room from windows across the front and one side. Some badly worn sheers hung in uneven bunches. Furniture and nicknacks had been removed from boxes and the boxes left piled in the far end of the entry as if someone had been interrupted in his work. Penny put her purse down, walked to the windows, and straightened the curtains. Then she picked up her grandmother's needlepoint chair and placed it at the left edge of the massive fireplace. Her hand trembled as she ran her fingers tenderly over the chair's hand–carved wooden frame. She laughed and sheepishly wiped a tear from her eye. "It really is beautiful."

Rich felt relieved. Looking at the bare hardwood floors, he said, "We'll have to do with what we have for a while, but we'll be able to get carpeting soon, and other things . . . "

"Oh, no, Rich. Not on these beautiful floors. Rugs, maybe." She turned until she had taken in all there was to see. Then she put her arms around Rich and hugged him tightly. "It's perfect," she pronounced.

"Welcome, neighbors," came a voice from the entry hall.

Rich turned back toward the front of the house and greeted a small aging man.

"Sam, isn't it?" Rich asked as he took the man's hand.

"Yes. Sam Farrell," the man replied. "It's nice to see you again."

"Honey," Rich said, putting his arm around Penny's shoulder, "this is Sam. Sam and his wife live next door."

"My wife's on her way," he said as he greeted Penny. "She had some—"

"Here I am." Mrs. Farrell stepped through the open door. She carried a large picnic basket in her arms and handed it to Rich. "Reverend Callahan, Mrs. Callahan," she said, nodding to each in turn.

"How nice this is!" Penny said. "Thank you very much."

Penny looked closely at the attractive older woman, her first friend in a community of strangers. She removed the cloth covering the basket and relished the aroma of freshly cooked chicken and homemade rolls. "This is wonderful," she repeated.

"What a day," Rich exclaimed as he fell into bed several hours later.

"A wonderful day," Penny agreed.

"You like the house? You really like the house?" Rich teased.

"Yes, I really like the house! You done good," Penny teased back.

They relaxed against their pillows and stared happily up at the ceiling.

"Rich." Penny turned suddenly on her side and looked at him. "I heard you ask Sam what that disturbance was down the block. Did he know?"

Rich shifted his pillow for more comfort and sighed thoughtfully. "Yes. It's the Women's Health Center. Pro–lifers were picketing."

"Right sympathies, wrong tactics."

"Exactly."

"Is there any hope in suggesting you not get involved?"

Rich turned toward her. "Are you serious?"

"I guess not. I'd just hoped we'd get away from all of that here."

"I know," he sighed, kissing her good night. "I know."

_____Five

The teakettle whistled shrilly and Rich removed it from the burner so he could be heard. "Listen to this," he said. He read aloud from the Chamberlain morning paper.

"The public is being misled by the radical activist groups that label the Women's Health Center an abortion clinic. The health center programs include a variety of family planning and health care services for women."

Penny listened intently as she stirred oatmeal for her family's breakfast.

"This statement came in answer to anonymous threats made against the center and its administrators. 'We're obviously providing needed service, as evidenced by the number of people taking advantage of our programs,' Mr. Benning, the center's director, said. There are more patients than the center can reasonably care for. The center plans to expand its services and hopes to supplement the already overworked staff with volunteers from the community. They need the help of qualified local professionals willing to cover every aspect of the services they provide, from the clerical to medical, including counseling."

Rich read on in silence. The article explained that while the Supreme Court ruling of twelve years earlier had denied the states and local governments the right to prohibit abortions, it had left them free to control the business of providing those and related services. Nebraska had passed some restrictions controlling abortions, and the Women's Health Center, a privately funded institution, had added to those regulations. There was one restriction that particularly interested Rich. The center, which had several offices around the state, required every patient to receive counseling before submitting to an abortion.

The patient could choose to get private counseling, but the paperwork involved with proving proper accreditation, etc., was so mind-boggling that most of the patients chose the free services provided by the center. That was where the women's center could use some volunteers.

Rich put the paper down, lost in thought as he sipped his coffee.

"You still with us?" Penny asked as she put his breakfast in front of him.

Rich smiled as he watched his wife put their pajama-decked toddler into his high chair.

"Sorry, I guess I was somewhere else. Can I help with something?"

"No, we're all set."

Rich looked around the large oval table surrounded by his young family and smiled again. The children were each at different stages of dress. Bobby was tying his shoes, Caroline looked properly neat and ready for the day, Timmy needed to comb his hair and his shirt was buttoned wrong, Rachel had gotten her pj's off and sat at the table in her underwear, and the baby — well, he was just the baby. Tomorrow, Rich resolved to himself, he would help with the children while Penny cooked.

"Bobby, how about you say grace this morning?" their father asked.

"Sure," the boy said, folding his hands in front of him.

Rich uttered a silent prayer as he faced the row of chanting picketers that still surrounded the clinic's front walk when he approached its entrance later that day. Their faces all wore the same angry scowl. They walked slowly in a circle, crossing back and forth over the center's front walk and making it impossible for him to enter unnoticed. "Every life is precious" and "Your baby has a RIGHT to life" were the two signs he saw first. He couldn't argue with that. Another had a picture of an aborted fetus, tiny and scorched red with saline solution. Rich cringed and looked away. The air was warm for January. Rich had worn his heavy coat but had left his scarf at home. Realizing his white clerical collar gave him away, he wished he'd worn the scarf.

"Where you going, Reverend?" a large woman asked, resting her sign on the ground in front of her.

Rich took a deep breath and then spoke slowly. "I have business inside."

"What business would a preacher of God have in this place?" came another.

Rich was humbled by the thought of the Savior and the company he chose to keep, the thought of His going out into the streets to comfort blind beggars and tell stories to thieves and prostitutes. " 'They that be whole need not a physician, but they that are sick,' " Rich was about to answer, when a dark young woman stepped out of a car at the curb and began her walk up from the street. The driver waited only a second, then the car door slammed shut and he sped away, spraying the picketers with ice and mud.

"Don't kill your baby," the group began to chant. The heavy woman who had first spoken to Rich, the leader of the group, he supposed, approached the frightened girl and asked with contrived sweetness, "Are you here for an abortion?"

The girl appeared confused and didn't answer. "I, uh . . . who are you? I don't have to answer . . . "

Rich watched the scene closely.

The woman stamped snow from her boots, put her sign down at her feet, removed her mittens, and pulled a pamphlet from her coat pocket. It had the same bloody picture on the front that her sign displayed. Rich stepped forward and took the girl's arm.

"You're right, of course. You don't have to answer any of these people's questions." He held her trembling arm firmly against his body and walked her inside.

"You're helping to kill babies, Reverend," he heard the woman shout from outside as the door closed behind him.

As he and the young girl entered the sparsely decorated office from the Fifth Avenue entrance, Rich wondered at the number of women who were sitting there. The center's waiting room, which was probably fifteen feet square and was lined with folding chairs, was filled to capacity. A medicinal smell hung in the air the way the smell of liquor lingers long after a party has ended. Large green plants in plastic pots stood in two corners. Magazines lay askew on a plastic table. Rich helped the girl with her coat and hooked it on a rack near the door along with his own.

"Thank you," she said before he had a chance to speak. Her face was clear of makeup and deeply lined for someone obviously young. Her eyelids were red and her nose raw and chapped.

"You're welcome. I'm Reverend Callahan. If I could help you in some way, I'd like the opportunity."

"No. Thanks again. I'll be all right now that I'm inside. I am glad I didn't have to run that alone."

Rich wondered about the man he'd only partly seen who'd left her there. "If you'd like to talk, sometimes a sounding board can clear things up that seem—"

"No, thanks, really."

She looked straight at him, and the timidity he had detected there before was gone. He backed away.

"I'll announce you to the receptionist," he offered.

"That's okay. I have an appointment. They know I'm here."

The girl at the desk was slow to wait on him. He was about to inform her that he only had a question, when she finally acknowledged his presence and asked what he wanted.

"I'm Richard Callahan. I'm the pastor of the Chamberlain Community Church on State Street." The shapely woman wore pants that were too small and a shirt that was too big. She took a piece of gum from her mouth and tossed it into a waste-basket. She shuffled through some papers on her desk, apparently searching for something. "I've come in answer to your ad for volunteers." His voice went up at the end as if it were a question.

"Oh, yes. Mr. Callahan, was it?" Her voice was flat and nasal. He was surprised she had caught his name. "Please have a seat. Mr. Benning will see you as soon as he can."

He waited for nearly an hour. Women of various ages disappeared behind the door that separated the waiting room from whatever lay beyond it. A pale, tired-looking young woman, almost a child herself, was brought out through that door in a wheelchair, still groggy from anesthetics, and was helped into a waiting car by a friend or relative taking her home to recuperate.

The interview with the center's director went about as Rich Callahan expected. Mr. Benning was neither friendly nor hostile. He smoked incessantly, grinding out one half-smoked cigarette and lighting another. It was apparent that he did not want the minister's services in his clinic. But, due to regulations he had no control over, he had no choice but to accept help as graciously as possible.

"You know, Mr. Callahan, that your counseling must be as impartial and unbiased as you can manage. The counselors here are required by law to present all the options available to the women who come here for help. Of course, what is said between you and a patient is confidential." He took a long draw on his cigarette, then tapped ashes into the glass tray. As he spoke he exhaled smoke from between his teeth. "But if you're ever accused of not presenting all the alternatives positively, you will be asked to leave."

Richard wondered if those counselors who were pro-abortion were given the same charge. But he cound manage that requirement without compromising his principles.

"Do you understand that?"

"Yes, I understand."

"Good," Benning said as he signed Richard Callahan's application and resume. Handing him a small pamphlet and a mimeographed sheet, he said, "Read these. The booklet explains all our services. The other sheet lists the options the law requires you to present to each patient you see. Stop at the front desk. The girl there will show you our work schedule. Fill in as many of the blank spaces as you can." The administrator rose from his chair and offered his hand to the young minister. "We'll see you — probably next week."

Taking his hand, Richard responded, "Yes. Thank you." And he left.

He signed up for four hours during each of the next two Mondays, since Monday was one of his days off. He'd give that much time a try and see how he handled it before he committed himself to more.

Six

Jeff pulled his sweatshirt down over his head as he bounced off the last step of the stairs that led into his in-laws' oversized kitchen. The old house Maggie had grown up in fascinated him. It was the only house he'd ever been in with two stairwells — one near the front door next to the large entry and a narrower one in the back. The house had been the center of a large farm in one of the many small communities that surround the San Francisco Bay area. The town had grown out and eventually encompassed it. The thick walls kept it warm in the winter and cool in the summer. The kitchen itself was big enough to accommodate a large oval oak table with ten chairs around it. A breakfast bar had been added when the two ground floor bedrooms were opened up and converted into the family room. It didn't surprise him that Maggie loved to come back here whenever she could. Her parents lived here, of course, but besides that, the house itself exuded warmth that made its occupants feel at home.

Jeff pulled the hem of his shirt down over the elastic waist of his running shorts and turned toward the refrigerator. He had one hand on the fridge door when a scene outside caught his attention. Maggie and her sister Gretchen were sitting in a wicker settee under the shade of a giant elm tree. A nest of oriole fledglings hung from one of the upper branches. The mother bird stood guard as each of her little ones peeked out through the nest's tiny hole. It was January already, and the young ones were nearly as large as their mother. Jeff wondered at the mother's watchful care as her children took off on expert wings. Their noise and activity went unnoticed by the two sisters below.

Maggie leaned her head against the backrest of the settee and pulled her sweater tightly around her. Gretchen sat with one arm around her sister's shoulder and rested gentle fingers on Maggie's forearm. Jeff stood still for a long moment watching. Tension began to build in his midsection and he stretched both arms suddenly above him in an effort to shake it off. Then, with a deep breath, he dropped his arms to his sides, rolled his shoulders vigorously backward, and forced his eyes away from the back window.

"You know what that's all about?" a full baritone voice asked from the family room. It was Carl, Gretchen's husband. Jeff finished pouring himself a glass of milk and ducked back into the fridge to put the milk away.

"I could give a good guess," he sighed without looking up.

"Maggie looks pretty upset."

Jeff finished his milk quickly, rinsed out the glass, and put it in the sink.

Carl waited for a response, then said, "Hey, you don't have to tell me . . . "

"You're right. I don't." Jeff reached for the back doorknob, then thought better of it and turned toward the front of the house. Carl stood motionless, staring at him. Jeff felt his shoulders sag. "Look, Carl, why don't you ask Gretchen when she comes in. I'm going running, in case anyone asks." He left quickly before Carl could say anymore.

Jeff ran north along the narrow curbless street, away from town. Within a block he was past the last house and facing endless rows of grapevines tangled in wire mesh. The road ahead of him disappeared, then reappeared as summits were reached. He picked a spot on the horizon he knew to be half his desired distance and marked it in his mind. It was warm for January. The sun was bright and bore down on him. The thick, humid air seemed to rub against his skin as he moved through it. Within minutes he shed the sweatshirt. Without stopping, he pulled it up over his head and down the length of his arms. He stuffed an edge of it under the back waistband of his shorts and let it dangle behind him.

He laughed as he thought of what Maggie would say. She was right. He enjoyed suffering. The wet, sticky perspiration that ran down his face and body and gathered in pools under his eyes and at the back of his knees annoyed him. But every time he ran he felt every muscle in his body contract and relax in perpetual rhythm. Tension stored in them, due to forces he couldn't control, was released, and he took charge again. After a time, exhaustion would take hold of him, requiring him to draw on reserves of strength most people don't know they have. Soon the fatigue would pass and he'd feel he could run on forever. That was why he ran. But he tried to be sensible about his running. He limited his runs to 10K in cool weather and less on hot days. Otherwise his body would suffer. And he ran every other day—a pace meant to maintain conditioning rather than increase it.

When he reached the point he'd determined to be halfway, he turned and headed back toward home. As his body took on a new surge of energy, his mind cleared and his thoughts returned to Maggie. He felt relieved to see her confiding in her sister. He hoped she would do the same with her parents. Gretchen was a spunky lady. If anyone could help Maggie through this, it was she. He felt a little pang of guilt over the scene with Carl. He knew Carl was hurt over it, and the mystery he'd added to the situation would only make Carl more curious. He guessed he felt that, since this was Maggie's family, she should be the one to tell them.

That thought brought back memories of his family. He'd been almost glad that the play that had claimed his and Maggie's lives over the past three years had ended. He'd found work on the West Coast which forced them to leave New York and his family again. Just before they left, his mother and sisters had been so obsessed with his and Maggie's problem that he'd felt compelled to tell them to mind their own business. That scene had brought torrents of tears, and his father had come down hard on him for hurting his mother. Maggie hadn't wanted to share their grief with anyone, and his family's meddling had only increased the tension between them. Jeff shook his head and sent perspiration in a fanlike spray out behind him. The fight had ended, fortunately, not long before they had left New York . . .

"Pop, this is none of your business," Jeff insisted, grateful that none of his sisters were there. His mother sat in a corner alone, dabbing her eyes with a damp handkerchief. Maggie had escaped to the kitchen. The small apartment where he and his six sisters had grown up felt crowded with just the four of them.

"What do you mean, it's none of our business? We're your family." Jeff's father was a large man in his early sixties with the body and strength of someone much younger. He ran a small neighborhood grocery store and still unloaded delivery trucks of canned goods and fresh produce. The work had kept him young and vigorous. He'd never raised a hand against any of his children, and yet the sheer massiveness of his body had kept Jeff in line all those years of growing up, even without threats. He frowned at Jeff and turned toward a window.

"What's so terrible?" his mother asked. "We're concerned about you and Maggie. You're wasting important years." She rose from her chair and faced him squarely. "Think of Maggie. The older she gets the harder it will be on her." Jeff felt the scowl on his face and did nothing to change it. "Don't look at me like that. I'm your mother." She returned his scowl and Jeff stuffed his hands in his pockets and moved back a step. His mother was tall but thin and frail. She used her unique combined appearance of strength and weakness to her advantage whatever the circumstance. At one moment she could be weak and submissive, and her husband would jump to her rescue. In the next breath she could pull herself to her full height and command attention from anyone.

Jeff's retreat from her gave him new perspective and he advanced again. "What's so terrible, Mama? I'll tell you what's so terrible. You make us miserable asking us personal questions about our lives together."

His mother stood her ground. "A baby, Jeff. That's all we want from you. I know what the world teaches today — wait. Wait until you've had a career. Wait until you've had your fun. Wait until you've experienced life." Jeff threw his hands in the air, turned away from his mother's gestures, and slumped into a chair. "You listen to me," she continued. "This *is* life, and you're missing it. You wait too long and it'll be too late. By the time your papa was your age, he had . . . "

"I know. I've heard it all before." Jeff stretched his long legs in front of him and with his toe absentmindedly poked at the pleated skirt of an old footstool. His mood now was flat and feelingless, and he wished he and Maggie could escape. With that thought he stood suddenly and reached for his coat. When he looked up again, Maggie stood at the kitchen door. She held a paper napkin in one fist, and with the other she tried to smooth the wrinkles out of her rumpled dress. Her colorless face looked calm while her hands jerked and twisted at their contrived task.

She stood there wiping feverishly at her skirt and focusing on nothing. In a moment she stood erect and spoke directly toward Jeff as if she were talking to him. "We can't." Her voice boomed and surprised everyone.

"What?" Jeff's father asked, breaking the long silence.

Jeff took a deep breath and held it for a moment. When he finally let it go, he felt fifty pounds lighter. The room was silent. "We've tried, Pop. We haven't given up yet. There are still a couple of options left. We've just kept hoping it would all be solved before . . . we should have told you a long time ago. I'm to blame. I'm sorry."

He stepped close to Maggie, took her in his arms, and pressed his lips against her ear. "Finally. It's said," he whispered.

The old familiar house came into view again as he passed the last of the grapevines. Jeff cringed a little as he thought of surviving the same scene again, this time with Maggie's parents. He hoped they were still out shopping. He needed a shower and some time alone with Maggie.

He passed the folks' sedan in the driveway and jogged up the back steps and into the kitchen. Maggie and her sister were no longer in the backyard. The kitchen was empty. A large can of baked beans held down a stack of folded shopping bags on the counter, and a box of canned goods waited on the table for someone to put them away.

Jeff took a couple of paper towels off the roll near the sink and wiped the perspiration off his face and neck. The kitchen felt cool after his run, and he relished the feeling for a moment until his heart slowed and his breathing returned to normal. He heard voices coming from the living room. He wiped the towels across his damp head and ran his fingers back through his hair. He headed toward the voices. Catching a glimpse of himself in the entry mirror, he stopped long enough to slip his soggy shirt back on. Then he stepped around the corner to find Dr. and Mrs. Barnett talking with Carl and Gretchen.

"Nice run?" Dr. Barnett questioned the instant he saw Jeff.

"Fine, thanks. Is Maggie around?" Jeff looked at Gretchen, then Carl, hoping for some insight into what was happening here.

"We haven't seen her," Mrs. Barnett said.

"She's upstairs. I believe she's looking for you." Gretchen's eyes were wide and sad, and she smiled knowingly.

"I told Carl where I was."

"And I told her. That's when she went upstairs."

Jeff took the stairs two steps at a time, peeling his shirt off as he went.

He found her lying on the bed staring at the ceiling. She stood as soon as he came into the room. "Oh, hi," she said, smiling. "I didn't hear you come in last night. How'd the show go?"

Jeff looked at her closely. He'd intended to comfort her, but this facade of hers confused him. He mentally shrugged and tossed his shirt into the hamper next to the closet. "Fine," he answered. "I'm glad I didn't waken you."

"I'm not." She moved close, wrapped her arms around him, and rested her head on his chest. Then she backed away. "You're kind of . . . moist." Her nose wrinkled and the corners of her mouth turned down. She held her arms limply away from her as if she felt contaminated. He laughed. "Try 'smelly,' too. I'm about to take a shower." He opened a drawer, took garments from the top of the pile, and stepped into the bathroom. He heard her lie back down on the bed.

Jeff hurried through his shower. In a moment he finished, dried himself, and stood blow-drying his hair. He sensed movement in the doorway and turned to see her standing there. "The folks are excited about seeing you perform tonight," she said. "It'll be the first time."

The last of her comment was unnecessary, and he stopped to look at her. She was leaning against the door frame, with her thumbnail in her mouth, and was staring past him at nothing. "You all right?"

"Huh? Oh, yeah."

Jeff unplugged the dryer and coiled the cord around it. "I saw you talking with Gretchen this morning, before I left for my run."

"Oh!"

"Oh?" He stepped past her and pulled a pair of Levi's and a plaid sport shirt from the closet. "You going to make me guess what you were talking about?"

"You know what we were talking about."

"Good. It's about time your family knew."

"They don't know . . . yet. Gretchen promised she wouldn't tell."

Jeff stopped. "What? Maggie, don't do this."

"I know, I know. I've got to tell them. I'm just afraid it'll worry Mom."

"Your dad's a doctor, for pete's sake; he can help. And your mom'll worry more if she thinks you—we—don't want kids." Maggie's attitude angered Jeff. It had caused a temporary rift between him and his parents, and it was hurting hers, too. He shook his head as he sat on the edge of the bed away from her. He bent down and pulled on his socks.

"I wish now we'd told them sooner." Maggie looked pale and solemn.

Jeff thought of all the tests and all the treatments they'd been through, each one sure to work. Or so they thought. There hadn't been a logical time to inform their families. Each new test and treatment had been another reason to wait just one more month with the hope of delivering good news instead of bad. It had lengthened into more than a year without their wanting it to. He understood Maggie's hesitancy. Telling them now seemed anticlimactic.

"Telling my folks lifted a ton off me. You'd feel better about the whole thing if you'd . . . "

"I know, Jeff, I know." Maggie threw herself backwards onto the bed, stretched her arms above her head, then relaxed. "I really don't want to talk about this."

"It's a good thing our parents aren't closer," Jeff said as he tied the laces of his Topsiders. "Yours would be brokenhearted if they knew we'd confided in mine and not them. They'll have to know eventually."

"Not if we get pregnant."

"This is childish and that's a big if."

"It's not childish . . . "

"It is childish. You act as if we have something to be ashamed of."

"You know that's not true. It's just very private. And it'll happen. If it doesn't, they'll understand."

"They deserve better."

"They're my parents."

"And they deserve better." He felt angry as he took hold of the doorknob.

"You're right. I am going to tell them," Maggie whispered.

Jeff released his grip on the door and let his head fall against it with a loud thud. Then he turned back to see her still leaning against the door. "When?" he asked.

"Right now," she answered.

He slid sideways to clear the door and pull it open for her.

"How can we help?" Dr. Barnett responded once the truth was revealed to him. The family patriarch looked undisturbed as he hugged his daughter with one arm and gently gripped Jeff's shoulder with the other.

Maggie had struggled at first to say the words, but now that it was done, she appeared extraordinarily relaxed. Jeff took a deep breath and squeezed her hand.

Mrs. Barnett took Maggie's other hand and, when her husband's embrace ended, drew her daughter onto the couch next to her. "Yes, we'd like to help."

Gretchen and Carl had left just before Maggie and Jeff came downstairs. Jeff had heard their car pull onto the country road moments before the small talk turned serious. He felt glad — this was complicated enough.

How can we help? Jeff repeated his father-in-law's response over again in his brain, wondering at its simplicity. Yes, that was what they needed — help. He laughed, and everyone's attention turned toward him.

"I, ah . . . I was just thinking about how you can help. You've done that already. This could've been . . . well . . . it has been difficult. You folks make it easier. We should've told you sooner. We've got one or two options left to us. We haven't given up. I guess all that's left for others to do for us is pray. We can use all of that we can get."

Seven

The Fifth Wheel, a popular night spot in San Francisco, featured deejays most nights, but occasionally engaged small groups to perform in person. The group that had hired Jeff worked mostly in the L. A. area. Their agent had gotten them a gig at The Fifth Wheel—a good sign. It meant they were catching on. They wanted to branch out to other audiences. It had made Maggie especially happy, since her parents lived nearby. She had assured Jeff that they'd be welcome to stay there, and Jeff could commute to the city.

People were already packing the standing-room-only section when Maggie arrived at the club. Jeff watched from the control booth at the ceiling's edge above the dance floor. With her were her parents, Gretchen and Carl, and two other sisters — Penny and her husband, who lived in San Francisco, and Clarisse, who lived with her young family further north. Bringing her baby with her, she had come down for a few days to visit with Maggie, while her husband and other children remained at home.

Jeff saw Maggie hand the reservations clerk the business card he'd scribbled a note on. He felt a rush at the sight of her and laughed at himself because of it. After his knowing her four years and after almost three years of marriage, she could still make his pulse race. She wore a pair of black silk evening pants, pleated at the waist and at the ankles, and a shiny black sweater knit from narrow satin ribbon instead of yarn. It was studded with a swirl of sequins that began just above the ribbing at the right waist and extended in a wide sweep across her up to the left shoulder. Her natural curls in the dim light appeared the same color as the sweater. She'd pulled them straight back from her face and tied them in place with a single rhinestone strand. The effect was a halo of light surrounded by a ring of soft curls. He felt his heart take another leap as he imagined he could smell her favorite perfume. A waiter led them to a large table at the edge of the dance floor.

In the middle of the floor and elevated four feet above it stood the stage. It was a round platform fifteen feet in diameter that rotated clockwise very slowly. On nights when there was no live entertainment, people danced on it. Tonight it was covered with mikes, amps, cables, and instruments.

The dance floor was made of clear colored acrylic through which lights shined from below. The mosaic-like acrylic squares were arranged to appear as a huge wheel, the stage forming the hub. Black, purple, and dark blues combined to represent the sidewalls and tread. White opalescent tiles were the whitewall. And the words "Fifth Wheel/Top Forty" stood out in a bright fuchsia against the dark sidewalls. The floor was stationary, but the movement of the lighting directed against the outside walls coordinated perfectly with the movement of the stage and gave the impression that it was the floor that was turning. Jeff laughed as he watched members of Maggie's family blink and rub their eyes, looking first at the walls, then at the stage. He'd reacted the same way the first time he saw it. It took a minute to get used to the effect. Fortunately, it didn't move fast enough to make anyone dizzy.

"And now, ladies and gentlemen," the deejay began. Jeff left his place at the window and scrambled down the narrow spiral stairs to the room where George and the others waited to go on. He nodded to George as he took a deep breath, held it for a moment, then let it out slowly as the announcer continued. He felt giddy, another sensation he wondered if he'd ever grow out of. He'd been a professional entertainer for nearly ten years, and he still suffered stage fright. "We interrupt our music from the top forty to introduce to you a group new to the Bay Area. They've dazzled audiences to the south of us for more than a decade, and The Fifth Wheel is proud to bring them here for their San Francisco debut. Let's welcome some mellow fellows who'll swing and sing your favorite tunes — A nice round of applause for George's Regulars!" The audience cheered loudly. George led the group as they ran along through the crowd on a path cleared for them by the waiters. They were well into their first number when the applause finally stopped. Their costumes bore a 1776 theme. They were such a ragtag bunch that Maggie said they looked more like pirates than revolutionaries. George wore a three-cornered hat, a ruffled shirt, jacket heavy with gold braid and epaulets, and high-top boots. Jeff wore the ruffled shirt, open at the neck, and boots, but no hat or jacket. His pants were navy blue, the legs stuffed into the tops of his boots. The other three were similarly dressed. Their haircuts were what brought their look back to the present. Jeff's was cut medium short, lengthening out into a shag in the back that overlapped the top of his collar. For concerts he moussed it, combed it back at the sides and straight out everywhere else, not in spikes but evenly round, like a large pompom. The other fellows looked even scruffier. The lead guitarist wore a patch over one eye. Maggie was right. All they needed was one to wear a peg leg and a hook, and their look would be complete.

The stage lights kept Jeff from seeing the audience sitting at their tables, but he could dimly see them on the dance floor. He looked for Maggie and saw her several times as she danced with her dad and her brothers-in-law. He saw her dancing a couple of times with a tall stranger, and surprised himself with pangs of jealousy. Not that he was worried, he told himself, but he'd surely like to be the one to hold her.

Tonight they had played two sets. The family had come for the second, at eleven. When it ended after midnight, Jeff rushed to be the first back to their dressing room. He quickly scrubbed the makeup from his face, showered, dressed, and hurried out to the dance floor. The deejay was back into his routine, and Maggie was dancing with Carl. Jeff cut in.

The deejay played a slow, romantic song, and Jeff tightened his hold around Maggie's waist. Her hair emitted a fresh fragrance that drew his face into it.

"You guys were great."

"The music wasn't too wild for your parents?"

"It's not their taste, of course, but they were impressed with the audience's reaction to you. And the rest of us liked it. Clarisse is now your biggest fan." She laughed. He laughed with her.

She pulled back and looked more closely at him. "You washed your hair. How come?"

"You think your folks go for the 'finger in a light socket' look?"

"I like your hair that way. It's chic and up-to-date."

"So you've said."

"So? Don't I count?"

"Oh-ho," he laughed. He moved his hand up to just below her shoulder blades, drew her closer, and pressed his lips to her forehead. He felt her left arm tighten around his neck.

Maggie reached an arm down around Jeff's neck and kissed him on the top of the head as he sat relaxing at the folks' home a couple of hours later. "Here," she said, handing him a frosty mug filled with ice cream and overflowing with foamy root beer.

"Thanks." He took her hand and held onto it until she came to sit beside him on the sofa. Clarisse sat next to her and Gretchen pulled a chair in close enough that their knees almost touched.

"Mom." Clarisse leaned back and called toward the kitchen. She moved the throw pillow next to her and patted the cushions of the couch. "Come in here with us. We've got room for one more."

"How about two more?" Mrs. Barnett came into the room carrying Clarisse's six-month-old son, Jeremy.

"I didn't hear him. Was he crying?"

"That's for a grandma to know and a mother *not* to find out."

"Mom, you'll spoil him."

"Also a grandma's privilege."

Carl and Dr. Barnett laughed together. Jeff felt Maggie sit up straighter and turn toward her sister. He put his left arm behind her along the back of the couch and touched her shoulder with his thumb. She was staring intently at the baby's face. She leaned back against him. "Isn't he darling, Jeff?"

Jeff took the last swallow of ice cream and root beer and set the mug and napkin on the table next to him. "Yes, he is."

"Would you like to hold him?" Clarisse asked.

Gretchen frowned and moved to take the baby when Maggie answered.

"Oh, Yes! Please."

Once the baby nestled in her arms, she settled back against Jeff again. The smell of baby and talcum mingled with Maggie's perfume and blended into a fragrance that warmed him. She loosened the blanket from around Jeremy's legs. He wore a blue-and-white striped knit sleeper that looked like a baseball uniform. It had pulled up in back until the baby's legs were bound up next to his body. Maggie gently tugged on each legging and lengthened it out so he could kick freely. Then she rewrapped the blanket around him loosely and drew him close to her. Mrs. Barnett handed her a bottle of warm milk.

"Clarisse, I thought you nursed all your babies," Maggie commented.

"I did the others, and Jeremy for a while. I got tired of being the only one who could feed him. The older kids love to help, you know. I figured I ought to take advantage of that."

"Oh, I'd *want* him all to myself," Maggie cooed as she gave the baby the bottle.

"You say that now, but wait till you have one of your own — no — four or five of your own."

Jeff felt Maggie stiffen. He tightened the fingers of his left hand around the back of her neck and massaged her gently. He wished they'd had a chance to tell the whole family of their problem. Clarisse was still in the dark, and he could see this conversation taking a painful turn. Gretchen frowned again. "Let me take the baby, Maggie. I'm an old hand at this, you know."

Maggie looked hurt, and Gretchen cringed at what she'd said. She backed off. "I can handle it," Maggie said.

"I know you can. I only meant . . . "

Carl, who sat in a chair opposite Jeff and next to Dr. Barnett, leaned forward to speak to the two men. "What're you doing in the Church down home, Jeff?" he asked.

"I coach two teams of boys' basketball."

"That sounds more like fun than work."

"Yeah, I'm one of the lucky ones. I worry sometimes about the example I set for them. I mean, I'm a good guy, but I'm not perfect, and those boys watch me constantly."

"Gotta be sure you don't beat your wife in public, that kind of thing." Carl smiled broadly and Dr. Barnett winced.

Jeff laughed. "Exactly. It is fun, though. I wouldn't want to be doing anything else right now."

"Did I tell you about my Aaron's basketball prowess?" Carl continued. "He played junior varsity last year and has been practicing with the varsity team since school began. The coach just announced the lineup, and *my kid* made varsity. He's the only sophomore on the squad."

"That's great. He must be big for his age," Jeff responded.

"No, he's really not. But he's fast, Jeff. He slips in, grabs that ball from the bigger guys, and is halfway down the court before they know what hit 'em. You must have played basketball, since you're coaching now."

"Yeah, I did." Jeff looked back at the baby. Maggie made a clicking sound with her tongue and ran the tip of her index finger gently around his chin as he nursed. He stopped momentarily and smiled up at her. "Oh, what a happy boy," she cooed. He pushed the nipple out of his mouth with his tongue and made a soft gurgly sound like bubbles escaping from a milk carton. "Now you're going to talk to me." Maggie handed Jeff the bottle and touched the baby's dimpled chin. "Yes," she said as he continued to gurgle. "Sure, go ahead. Talk to me." When he stopped, she gave him an extra squeeze and put the bottle's nipple back in his mouth. Jeff pulled his attention away from the baby and back to his conversation.

"I played a little in college, too, but I never made varsity. I had to work— no time for practice. It was fun, though—that's the point."

"I don't know, Jeff." Carl laughed. "Playing and winning's right up there with having fun. Dad here could tell you about one game last year when Aaron and another boy . . . "

Jeff struggled to keep his attention directed toward the men, but his eyes kept turning back to the child in Maggie's lap.

"I'm sorry, Dad. What did you say?" he had to ask one time when his father-in- law directed a comment to him.

Dr. Barnett laughed. "Don't apologize. That boy who's got most of your attention is my grandson, after all. You go right ahead and fuss over him."

"He's a cute boy," Jeff said.

Clarisse laughed. "You know, to hear you two talk, I'd swear no one ever told you where babies come from. You can have one of your own, you can . . . ouch!" She leaned over suddenly and rubbed her left shin. The pointed toe of Gretchen's shoe had caught her squarely a few inches above her ankle.

"Sorry, Clarisse. I guess I moved too quickly." Gretchen rested her hand on Clarisse's knee but watched Maggie intently. "Are you all right?" she asked.

"I'll live," Clarisse answered, "but my stockings have had it." She fingered a run that slowly moved down toward her ankle.

Maggie nodded silently.

Dr. Barnett frowned and leaned back in his chair, his eyes trained on Maggie and the baby.

Jeff felt his throat tighten painfully. He wondered how Maggie was keeping the tears back. He waited a moment, hoping Maggie would take the opening to tell Clarisse their secret. When she didn't, he took hold of Maggie's neck again and firmly pressed his thumb and index finger against the hollows just below her hairline. "I hate to break up this party, but I've been working while you folks played, and I'm tired." He stood and watched Maggie swallow hard and gently roll the baby, who was now dozing, into his mother's arms.

"Thanks, Clarisse. That was fun."

Maggie stood, and Jeff took her shoulders in one arm and pulled her toward him. She stumbled off balance for a moment, then kissed him on the cheek and whispered "I'm okay if you're okay" into his ear. He nodded.

"Oh, you newlyweds," Clarisse said. "Life's such a happy game."

Jeff laughed, and directed Maggie quickly toward the stairs.

_____Eight

"Ralph, the girl doesn't need a new formal. She's got a closet full of formals." Marianne Renwick followed her husband into the playroom of their spacious suburban home. Cybil held the phone to her ear, waiting as it rang. She opened the door a crack so that she could watch her parents as they argued. Snow caked the panes of the double-glassed french windows across the back wall. A fire blazed in the fireplace. The room was warm and comfortable. Mr. Renwick put a record on the turntable and adjusted the speakers as music filled the room. "What do I tell her, we can't afford it? She knows better."

"You haven't been listening. She's being punished."

"You already said she could go to the dance."

"The dance, yes. But she's grounded until then. A shopping trip is out of the question. I told her no to a trip to town before she asked you. Why can't you see through her tricks? She uses you."

"So you've said. Look, I didn't agree to the punishment in the first place, and I definitely don't see why it has to exclude a new dress."

"Because I told her it did." Marianne picked up yesterday's newspaper from the coffee table and folded it in half with a snap. Ralph turned the volume up on the stereo, leaned back in his favorite recliner, and wrapped the headphones over his ears. His wife turned with a jerk and whacked him across the thigh with the folded paper on her way out of the room.

Cybil frowned. *If only they didn't fight*, she thought. She liked getting her way — who wouldn't? But she wished they wouldn't fight. She closed the door carefully and turned her attention back to the phone. "Julie? Oh, good. I was just about to hang up. I get it — the new dress!"

"Great! I got the car. I'll pick you up in ten minutes."

"No." Cybil checked her watch. "Give me half an hour exactly and call me back."

"What for?"

"Just do it."

Cybil dropped the receiver onto its cradle and pushed the phone to the back of her desk. She looked around her room and spent a moment of careful planning. It wouldn't take long to please her mom. It was worth the effort. She gathered the clutter of papers in front of her into an uneven stack and pushed them into one of her bottom drawers. The junk on top of her dresser went into another drawer. Then she opened her two top drawers and quickly smoothed out their contents. One contained nothing but underwear, the other, scarfs and gloves. She took a slip and panties from the one and folded them neatly and laid them across the top. In the other drawer she carefully placed neatly folded scarfs. She quickly stowed the clothes that littered her room in the hamper at the end of her bed. With a single yank she pulled her blankets up over her pillow. Another quick pull covered them with her thick comforter. *Thank goodness for the comforter. It'd hide anything*, she thought. She kicked at a corner of the blanket that hung below the quilt's edge and pushed it under the bed. *Now for the animals.* It took only seconds to arrange a half dozen of her stuffed toys across the lumpiest part of the bed to disguise the haphazard job. *There, Mom'll love it.* She could hear her mother working in the kitchen, so she went the long way through the living room and then through the kitchen to the back porch. Mrs. Renwick continued unloading the dishwasher as Cybil walked by her. "Got my room almost done, Mom. I need the vacuum."

"You know where it is."

Cybil hurriedly took the machine from the closet and dragged it across the narrow hall to her room. She ran the vacuum over the most visible sections of carpet, then left it running while she straightened shoes on the shelf in her closet and evened out the bunches of clothes on the rack. Clothing not on hangers, she gathered up and pushed into the hamper. When the lid wouldn't close she rearranged the top layer of clothing and pushed a little harder. "There," she said out loud as she heard the lid snap shut. Then she went into the bathroom and shoved jars and junk into the drawers. A quick swish made the sink and tub presentable. She grabbed up dirty towels and washcloths and dropped them down the laundry chute. *Adequate, adequate*, she thought as she perused her work. *It'll pass, and Mom'll eat it up.* She checked her watch. The time was just right. "Mom," she called.

"What now, Cybil?" Mrs. Renwick said as she opened her daughter's door. Cybil wound the cord up on the vacuum and casually leaned against it as she watched her mother's inspection tour. "Not bad," Marianne said coolly as she walked into the room and looked behind the door, then in the closet. "You could do a better job on the bed."

Cybil nodded humbly.

Marianne stepped sideways to the dresser and opened one of the top drawers. "Uh, huh." She looked at Cybil and shook her head. "Your gloss-over doesn't fool me, but I guess it's better than nothing. Next time straighten the middle drawers. I'll check there first."

"Yes, Mother." Cybil smiled soberly and handed the vacuum to her. Mrs. Renwick had turned the machine toward the door when the phone rang. *Right on cue, Julie*, Cybil thought. She picked up the receiver.

"Hello . . . oh, hi, Julie . . . I don't know. Mom's right here. Let me ask." She held her hand over the mouthpiece. "Julie's got her mom's car and . . . "

"You're grounded, Cybil."

"I know — but to get my dress. Dad says it's okay."

Mrs. Renwick took another look around her daughter's room. "Okay. I guess you've earned it — but three hours only. I want you home for dinner." Mrs. Renwick turned to leave.

"Uh, Mom? Money?"

"Talk to your dad."

"Thanks, Mom." Cybil smiled sweetly, hoping her mom would smile back.

"Right."

Cybil silently signaled for Travis to stay put in the hall outside her parent's room. Then she carefully opened the door and tiptoed to the bedside table where her father's alarm clock stood. She noiselessly held the "set" lever down and watched as the illuminated numbers ran through their cycle once and again; then she released the lever at 11:30 P.M. Once back in the hall, she led Travis into the kitchen, where she changed the electric clock to also read 11:30. Then she unplugged the VCR in the family room and plugged it back in. It flashed twelve. She also reset her alarm clock.

She giggled quietly once they were back on the front porch.

"I don't get it, Cybil. Your folks'll know you fiddled with the clocks as soon as they get moving in the morning."

"That's why I only changed the electric ones. They'll assume the electricity was off during the night — it happens — but they'll know it didn't happen before they went to bed, so I'm safe."

"What if they went to bed after 11:30?"

"Then I'm caught, but I'll take that chance. Nothing bad ever happens to me. You know that." Cybil tiptoed down the wooden porch steps, then laughed out loud and tromped back up them. "Oh, Travis, you're such a scream. I'll have to tell my dad that one, he'll love it." They went into the entry where they heard Mr. Renwick call to them. "Cybil, is that you? You're home early."

"I'm sorry, Daddy. I didn't mean to waken you. The dance is over. I just needed a warmer coat. We're going to get some ice cream, is that okay?"

"Home by one."

"Thanks, Dad." Cybil winked at Travis and led him back outside. Once safely in the car, they both laughed out loud. The car clock read 1:36 A.M. "Your dad's real dumb."

"He is not! He sees what he wants to see. I get caught often enough. He's just too kind . . . or something. But he's not dumb! Now let's get going to that party."

Cybil felt stupid sitting on the narrow wooden bench in the small town police station. The bouffant skirt of her formal took up half the bench. The room was full of cigarette smoke. The police wagon had just dropped off a load of drunks. The night officer struggled to keep them in line while they waited through the booking process. The smell of body odor and alcohol was nauseating.

While she waited she tried to imagine the route her father would take through the house after getting the call from the police. If he went to his dresser for his watch, she was doomed. He always parked his car in the driveway out front, so she knew he wouldn't go past the battery clock on the back porch; and the clock in his car hadn't worked since the warranty ran out. His watch was her only threat. She looked up in time to see her father come through the double doors across from her. The only clock in the room was by the entrance above his head. She had to stop him before he got all the way in and saw it.

"Oh, Daddy," she cried, running to him. She took hold of his left hand and patted his wrist—no watch, thank goodness. "Please don't be angry. I'm so sorry. I didn't know . . . "

A uniformed officer interrupted her and took her father's hand. "Mr. Renwick?"

"Yes."

"I spoke to you on the phone. You can take your daughter home. We didn't book her, but I'd be more careful of the company she keeps from now on. We picked her up with a group of known drug abusers—next time she won't be so lucky."

"Drugs? Cybil."

"Honest, Daddy, I didn't know." She cuddled closer to him.

"She wasn't using, Mr. Renwick. Otherwise we'd keep her overnight. But frankly, I don't think she's as innocent as she looks. Like I say, next time'll be a different story."

Cybil scowled fiercely at the officer, then turned a sweetened face to her father. "Daddy, it was a party. I didn't know until I got there what kind. Travis wanted to stay. What was I supposed to do?"

"You could've called."

"Oh, Daddy." She leaned against him and cried into his shoulder. "I know. I'm so ashamed, I just waited for it to be over." She looked sideways to see the officer mouth "Oh, brother!" and turn away.

"It's okay, Punkin." He had his face buried in her hair. "C'mon, your mother's worried. We'd best get you home."

"I'll know better next time, Daddy." Cybil flashed a smile back to the officer as she tucked her arm under her father's and followed him out of the door.

_____Nine

The kitchen was warm in spite of drafty floorboards and snow-caked windows. The cinnamon scent of cookies filled Rich's nostrils. He stepped through the hallway outside the kitchen and into the tiny room he used for an office, and he dropped his briefcase on the floor next to his desk. Books still lay in boxes waiting to be put away. He'd get to that soon, he promised himself.

"Penny?" He quickly picked up an array of toy trucks and blocks that littered the linoleum floor and put them in the box in the corner. "Where is everybody?" He got no answer, so he tracked down the source of the aroma he'd detected earlier and took a couple of cookies off the cooling rack next to the oven.

"Hands off, dear."

Rich stopped chewing and looked at his one remaining cookie.

"These were for something special?" he asked.

Penny smiled, then came into the kitchen and wrapped her arms around him.

"No, but you'll spoil your dinner."

"What dinner?" he asked, gesturing around the idle kitchen.

"I'm getting to it right now. You're earlier than I expected. How'd your day go?"

"Fine. The parish's governing board is a wild and crazy group."

"I'll bet."

"They want to meet you."

"I'll bet."

Rich laughed. "Well, like it or not, the ladies plan to take you out to lunch later this week."

"Later this week? They'd better let me know about it. I count only two more days left in this week, and I don't know anyone who can babysit."

"They have that one figured out."

"Really? Who?"

"Me."

They both laughed.

"Did you visit the center today?" Penny asked.

"Yes." Rich went to the fridge and poured himself a glass of milk.

"There's not much to tell. There were a lot of women there, but it was pretty obvious they weren't all there for abortions." Rich looked at his wife for a moment, then turned to sit at the kitchen table.

"Penny," he finally began. "You know I'm not going to cause any trouble. That's not my style."

"Then why not stay out of it?"

"I can't do that. I have to do what I can. These people have to know how I feel about abortion. If it's a touchy subject for them, then so be it. But I can't be silent."

"It was because you couldn't be silent that we had to leave California."

"I consider that a blessing, don't you?"

"Yes, but you were just lucky they let you resign. If they'd fired you, you'd never have gotten this position. And that one wasn't over abortion—it was environment."

"It's my duty to prick the consciences of those in power. That's my job." He shrugged and raised his eyebrows, hoping she'd understand this time, fearing she might not. He wanted her to smile at him.

"Even if those in power also sit on the church's board." She frowned.

"Especially if."

Rich looked closely at Penny. He pained at her expression. She wanted to stay here. He knew that. His attitude was a threat to that desire. He understood that, too. He sighed and brushed the cookie crumbs from the tabletop into the palm of his hand.

"Look, the director of the women's center is not a member of this parish, so we have nothing to worry about."

Penny filled a saucepan with water and put it on the stove. Her expression remained the same as she went about her task of preparing dinner. Rich watched as she removed potatoes from the bottom of the fridge and began to peel them.

"All I've done so far," he continued, "is volunteer to work four hours a week as a counselor. What's the harm in that?"

"Were the picketers still there?"

"Yes. I had to run the gauntlet to get inside."

"And back out again."

"And back out again. So what?"

"And you didn't say anything to anyone."

"I spoke kindly to a soul or two. That's also my job."

At last Rich saw her expression soften and warm into a smile. She wrapped arms around his middle and rested her head against his chest. "I love you," she finally said. "I'm proud of you, too. I wish I had your courage."

Rich tightened his arms around her. "You do fine. Remember who it was who said 'We'll make it' when I was ready to toss it all way back in school?" He gazed down at her. "Remember? You buoy me up. That's *your* job."

Rich decided to do some research into sources of help available to women who were pregnant but didn't want to be. He found that while abortion clinics like the women's center where he was to work were numerous, there were other organizations that could offer more positive aid.

He learned that the Catholic church spent hundreds of thousands of dollars a year providing services to unmarried pregnant women, and also that The Church of Jesus Christ of Latter-day Saints provided social services for those who needed it, along with low-cost adoption services to families who could give the otherwise unwanted children a home. Other churches had similar programs.

As he checked around he found that there were a few local doctors and hospitals who willingly devoted a certain percentage of their medical practice to those who could not otherwise afford their services—including maternity care. There were lawyers willing to do the same thing.

He spent the rest of Thursday and all day Friday calling everyone in the local directory that might be of help. It was a start, but it wasn't enough. He added what he'd found to the list of government agencies given him by Mr. Benning. In addition he decided that every woman he talked with would go home with his address and telephone number and with warm assurances that she could call him anytime she needed help.

The library was an invaluable source of information about the issue of abortion. He spent Saturday reading. He felt he knew the basics about the current law and related subjects, but he wanted to be certain of his facts so that he could speak wisely about the problem. Mostly, he hoped to find insight into feelings of young women who were pregnant and didn't want to be. The ten-year anniversary of the historic Supreme Court decision had made abortion a hot topic, and he found current information readily available. He left satisfied that he was at least adequately prepared before he went to work the following Monday.

Monday morning was dreary. The warmer weather the Callahans had enjoyed their first week in Nebraska had given way to a sudden dip in temperature. Since Saturday the thermometer hadn't risen above freezing, and on Monday snow was predicted.

Rich had given up his plan to walk to the center for his first day of volunteer service. He directed his car into a parking space some distance from the center's entrance. When he opened his door, a sudden gust of wind took his breath and he stopped for a second. He pulled his coat collar more tightly around his scarf-wrapped neck and then stepped out. He carefully walked across the new snow that was quickly covering the ground, and he wondered how long it would take before his southern California feet felt secure on the slippery surface.

The snow had accomplished one thing. There were no picketers waiting outside. They would come, though, he thought, later in the day when more people were out and about. Eight o'clock was a little early on a dark morning when the thermometer was stuck at fifteen degrees.

The receptionist had a list of appointments ready for him when he checked in with her. She showed him to a nearly empty office and left him there alone.

A green metal desk stood like a dinosaur in the middle of the room. Its top was bare except for a large green blotter, a pad of paper, a pencil box with a half dozen pens and pencils in it, and a box of facial tissues. Inexpensively framed cardboard paintings of fields of flowers and flocks of birds decorated the freshly painted celery green walls. A chair with wooden arms and legs and overstuffed seat and back cushions faced the desk. It was green also. Other chairs like it lined the back wall.

Rich pulled from his briefcase a picture of his family and a small plaque with a scriptural passage on it and set them on the desk. *Next time I'll bring flowers*, he thought. A small wooden bracket meant to hold a nameplate sat at the edge of the desk. The receptionist told him it would be another week before his plate arrived. He put the empty bracket into the desk drawer.

Within moments he heard a knock at the door, and the receptionist introduced him to an attractive young woman.

The center had scheduled appointments for him every half hour. *Not long enough*, he had thought. But the first woman's laconic responses to his questions told him how it would go. She stood and left within ten minutes.

These women don't really want to talk to me. They're just meeting the legalities, he thought. Rich knew he could refuse to sign the form and they'd have to stay, but what was the point? There were other counselors in the center. Women determined to have an abortion would simply make an appointment with one of them. If he couldn't reason with them, no one else could, either.

"I'm ready for the next one." Rich tried to sound more positive than he felt as he passed by the receptionist's desk after taking a short break.

"Your next appointment hasn't shown up yet," she said apologetically, shuffling the papers in front of her from one pile to another.

Rich retreated to the tiny office and sat, leaning back in his swivel chair and stretching his arms over his head. He stifled a yawn.

His shift was almost over. He'd seen seven women, and none had spent more than twenty minutes talking to him. None had changed her mind about her decision to abort her baby. *Well, Rich old boy, so much for soapboxes and worthy causes.* He felt the twinge of failure—an important failure compounded by his worry about delivering his first sermon next Sunday to strangers he'd only met en masse. His day would've been better spent preparing for Sunday. A muscle twitched painfully across the center of his forehead. He rubbed it absently. *You're wasting your time—wasting your time.* He checked his watch, then stood and reached for his coat.

The receptionist opened the door and directed a well-dressed middle-aged woman to the chair opposite his desk. She had a lace handkerchief doubled and twisted around her fingers. Thin traces of dry mascara streaked her cheeks. Matching darker streaks edged the creases in her handkerchief.

Rich hung the coat back on the rack and offered her his hand. She took it limply and then sat down. He pulled his chair up and opened the manila folder provided by the receptionist.

"Mrs. Jones?" he asked.

She nodded.

"You're married, then," he said.

"Yes, of course." She didn't seem offended by the question, but her eyes darted from his eyes to her hands to the file folder.

"But you want to have an abortion. Why?"

She stood and walked to the window, but didn't look out. "I'm too old for this. My family's grown."

"You have other children?"

"Yes. A son who's seventeen and a daughter fourteen."

"What're their names?"

The woman turned nervously and found her seat. "I . . . uh, I'd rather not say."

Rich looked at her file. The information she'd provided was minimal.

"Then your name isn't Jones, either," he said.

She looked up at him and searched his face for a moment. "No."

"Does your husband know about this?"

"Yes."

"He approves of the abortion?"

The woman began to cry. She wiped her tears with her soggy handkerchief, then stuffed it in her purse. Rich offered her the box of tissues from his desk. After a moment she answered. "He insists on it."

Rich's mind raced over her answer. *He insists on it . . . insists . . . insists.* She blew her nose and threw the wadded tissue into the wastebasket.

"Your being here is *his* idea," he said.

The woman stood again and took two more tissues. She held them in the palm of her hand and pressed them against her face, blotting tears and stifling sobs at the same time.

Rich felt her pain tear at him. *How can a man be so insensi . . . whoa there, Rich, boy, hang onto your objectivity*, he reminded himself, as he swallowed hard.

"I didn't say that." She remained standing with her back toward him.

Rich waited for her to continue. When she didn't, he decided to change the subject.

"Mrs. Jones," he began. "Why did you choose to come to the clinic instead of consulting your private doctor?"

"I can remain anonymous here. I live at the other end of town. No one will know."

"Your friends won't know?" he asked.

"No! How could I share this with them?"

"How can you not? And your children?"

"Harry's going to send them to visit their grandparents for the weekend."

"You—and your husband—have this all figured out."

She began to cry again.

"Except that it's not what you want," he added.

Rich leaned back in his chair absently, chewing on the end of his pen, and waited for her to control her tears. Finally he spoke. "Regret is a terrible adversary."

"It couldn't be worse than what I'm feeling now."

"What are you feeling?"

"Pain. The most incredible pain."

"Because you're pregnant?"

She didn't answer.

"Or because of the decision to abort your baby?"

She began to cry again, muffling the sound with the soaked tissues in her hand.

Rich poked the pen he'd been fiddling with back in the holder on the desk. He took a deep breath and felt his jaw tighten in anger. He rubbed his face with both hands. "Can I talk to your husband? Would that help?"

"I don't think so. He's determined." She turned and sat in one of the chairs nearby. "And anyway, he wouldn't talk to you. He won't come down here."

Rich felt his stomach tighten. "Perhaps I could go to him."

"No, no. That would just make him angrier."

"You can't do this. Not when you're so obviously opposed to it. You'd never forgive yourself. He can't ask this of you. If he understood that, I'm sure it would help."

"I spent all last weekend trying to make him understand. He said I'd be glad once it was over."

"Do you have the strength to oppose him?"

"I don't know," she said between sobs. "I've never tried."

Oppose him? C'mon Callahan, haven't you learned better than that? Right or wrong, this is her husband you're talking about.

"Do you have your appointment for the abortion yet?" he finally asked.

"Yes. It's this weekend—Friday afternoon."

"Then you have four days to decide. I'll sign your form, but please know that I'm available to you anytime." He stood and stepped around to the front of his desk. He thought carefully. There was one thing she had to understand before she left. "One of the side effects of an abortion," he began, "is mental anguish felt sometimes months or even years afterward. And this is from women who thought that's what they wanted." He put his hand on her shoulder as she turned toward the door. "I'm afraid," he added, "that you'll suffer more if you do this than you can imagine. Destroying your child won't save your marriage. It could be the end of it."

"Thank you, Reverend," she said, "but I'm not the one who needs convincing."

"Confront your husband with your feelings. Make him understand how important this is to you. Oppose him, for your own sake," he finally said. "And call me. Anytime."

_____ *Ten*

Sunday was to be the first time Richard Callahan would address his new congregation. He had been introduced the first Sunday he was in town, but the church's governing board had given him a free week to get his family settled before he was required to begin.

On Friday Rich pulled two or three books off the shelves in his office at the church. The spacious mahogany-panelled room, adjoining the altar and choir loft, was grander than he had expected. He ran his fingers over the smooth, fine wood of the desk in front of him. *Vanity*. He wondered if a less ornate setting might be more appropriate for a minister of one of Christ's parishes. *No matter*, he thought. *I can handle it*. And he smiled broadly.

"Two more days, Callahan," Rich began out loud. "Get your mind off yourself and onto your sermon or you'll be sorry come

Sunday." He opened his Bible and began making notes. He wrote: "On the Mount of Temptation Jesus resisted every effort of . . . "

The phone rang. Balancing the receiver between his ears and his shoulder, he continued to thumb through the book. "Reverend Callahan."

"Callahan, what the . . . blazes do you think you're doing?" an angry voice sputtered.

"Mr. Benning?" Rich asked. "I'm sorry, I'm lost. What . . . ?"

"Mrs. Jones, that's what. Does the name ring a bell?"

Rich put his pencil down and leaned back in his chair. "Yes sir, it does. What's the problem?"

"She's due here this afternoon for surgery. Her husband just called madder than . . . than . . . "

"It's okay. I get the picture. Mrs. Jones decided against the abortion." Rich smiled and rubbed damp eyes with his fingertips. She had taken a stand. She'd come through.

"As if you didn't know."

"No, I didn't know, but I am glad."

"Listen, Callahan. I told you if you didn't handle your job fairly you'd be out, and I meant it."

"Did Mrs. Jones complain?"

"No, but her husband is spitting nails."

"He's not my concern, nor yours."

"The clinic has to survive in this community. We have enough enemies without creating new ones from our friends! You're hanging by a thread, Callahan. Watch yourself."

"Mr. Benning, I'm sorry if I've upset you, but I am doing what I promised. My first concern is the welfare of the people I deal with. I'm opposed to abortion. But I'm not there to stop anyone from doing what they're set to do. I am determined, however, to help a few avoid making a terrible mistake. I'm convinced that Mrs. Jones would have suffered if she had destroyed her child. I'm glad I had a part in preventing that, and you should be, too."

"I repeat, Callahan. Watch yourself." And he hung up.

Rich dropped the receiver lightly into its cradle. He smiled. Mrs. Jones had been the chief recurrent petition in his daily prayers, and Rich took a moment to silently say, "Thanks, Lord." Between the two of them, they'd saved two lives that day, and

Rich felt buoyant. *Is this pride, and is it sinful?* he asked himself. *No*, he thought. *It's joy, without blemish, and thank God for it.*

Rich reached forward and ripped the top sheet off his notepad. The subject he'd chosen for Sunday's sermon seemed inadequate. He would begin again: "Some of us find ourselves in positions of dominion over others. Sometimes by design, sometimes not . . . "

Rich paced nervously in his office as he listened to the organ prelude. His sermon notes were arranged on the podium, so he had no chance to look them over one last time. He went over and over in his head the few words he'd prepared for his opening. The choir began to sing, and moisture gathered in the palms of both his hands and under his snug-fitting collar. When the singing stopped, he stepped through the door into the chapel and walked toward the podium.

He looked down at his congregation and smiled. Most of the faces were still unfamiliar. Penny and the kids were sitting in their assigned places on the front row. He smiled inwardly and felt some of his tension dispel.

"The congregation will sing from hymn number 128," he announced and stepped back from the microphone. As he sang, he looked out over the congregation for the few faces familiar to him. Their neighbors, the Farrells, were there. Mrs. Browning, the chairperson of the board of governors, sat on the front row across the aisle from Penny. He nodded amiably as his eyes greeted hers.

Then he caught the startled eye of someone familiar. She wasn't altogether happy to recognize him, although she smiled as he nodded to her. It was "Mrs. Jones," and she stood next to Harry Miller, one of the church's board members. His heavy arm rested across her shoulders. She clutched a handbag with both hands and twisted its straps nervously. His eyes lingered on her and he stopped singing for a moment. Now he knew her right name. She was Mrs. Miller. Virginia was the first name she had put on her form. That was probably right.

It was strange sharing this terrible secret with her. *Thou hypocrite* Rich thought: Harry Miller had come to church on Sunday, he'd dominated discussion at last week's church council meeting, and then in private he'd tried to force his wife to abort their child.

Rich forced himself to finish singing the last verse of the hymn. *How am I going to deal with this man?* he asked himself. *Not now, Callahan. Deliver your prepared sermon. Mount your soapbox if you feel you have to, but not now!*

The sermon he'd prepared took on new meaning.

"Some of us find ourselves in positions of dominion over others. Sometimes by design, sometimes not." He closed the notebook in front of him and looked directly into the congregation. "Whatever the source of that dominion, we must take care not to exercise it unjustly. For once we begin to force others to do evil, however disguised it might be, we tread in dangerous waters." He began his message calmly, but the feeling behind it enraged him and his voice came out with a force even he didn't recognize. He raised his right hand and gestured with strength toward his people. "The Lord will not hold those blameless who choose to lead His innocent ones astray." His fist crashed to the pulpit. The sermon was not exactly the one he'd prepared, but there was no stopping it. It flowed.

When it was finished, he stopped abruptly. His eyes filled with tears, and he felt humbled. The chapel filled with silence. Reading from Galatians, he finished quietly, " 'For, brethren, ye have been called unto liberty; only use not liberty for an occasion to the flesh, but *by love serve one another.*' In Christ's name. Amen."

"Hello, Harry." Rich took the man's hand and held it firmly. Harry Miller exhibited extraordinary courtesy, albeit reserved, and appeared to love and respect his wife and children. *Was it all carefully rehearsed?* Rich wondered. He hardly seemed the man his wife had described. Sunday morning had turned cold, and Harry pulled the wide-lapelled collar of his overcoat up around the back of his neck, giving himself a sinister look that suited him. Rich smiled, then nodded warmly to Mrs. Miller. "Penny," he said to his wife, who stood beside him on the church's front steps. "This is Harry and Virginia Miller."

"Hello, Reverend, Mrs. Callahan," Virginia said with enthusiasm. "I enjoyed your sermon. It gave me new strength."

She looked deeply into Rich's eyes. "Harry, this is the strangest coincidence," she said, taking her husband's arm.

Rich looked closely at Virginia Miller and recognized a sparkle he'd not seen before. He smiled and nodded approval for what she obviously intended to do.

"Reverend Callahan is the counselor I told you about."

Harry Miller stared at his wife in apparent disbelief.

Rich was still clinging to the man's hand, and Harry tugged on it until Rich released it.

"Virginia, I can't believe you'd—" Harry began.

"I had no idea . . . I didn't know, of course, that you were our new minister," she said to Rich. "I think I told you Harry and I spent last weekend in Aspen, so we missed the formal introductions."

"Yes, I understand," Rich replied.

It was strange, he thought again, sharing a terrible secret with this woman. It would not be much of a secret for long, he guessed, as the woman continued to talk.

"Oh, Reverend Callahan, Mrs. Callahan, we have the most wonderful news—you'll be the first to know. We're going to have another baby. Isn't that wonderful?"

"Oh, that is wonderful," Penny sighed.

"Virginia, I don't think this is the place . . . " Harry said.

As quickly as the scene had begun it ended.

"Thank you, Reverend," Mrs. Miller said quietly. "I feel wonderful. You were right. And don't worry, we'll survive—all of us."

Rich nodded and smiled. He looked back at Mr. Miller. The man was scowling fiercely.

Rich could tell it was not over for him. He was in for trouble. He looked at Penny, whose face was full of questions.

"What was that all about?" Penny asked, as soon as they were home and the children were busy setting the table.

"What?"

"Don't pretend . . . "

"Oh. The scene with the Millers. It's a long story, and I can't tell you everything." Rich pulled clean dishes off the shelf and handed them to Caroline while Penny sliced mushrooms into the salad.

Penny was accustomed to Rich's confidences, and Rich knew she really didn't want to hear anything not intended for her. But as open as Virginia Miller had been, he could see why Penny figured there had to be more he could tell her.

"Mrs. Miller came to me for counseling."

"I gathered that, but there's got to be more to it."

"I gave her some advice her husband didn't like. It's as simple as that."

"Her husband, who happens to be on the church's board."

"That's right."

"The husband whose looks could've killed."

"He's harmless."

"He's not harmless if he's a member of the board."

"Penny, don't worry about it."

"That's what you said a year ago when you had another board member arrested for illegally dumping toxic waste."

"I didn't have him arrested."

"You might as well have. He knew you opposed him."

Rich didn't reply. He looked calmly at Penny until she could no longer meet his gaze.

"This obviously has to do with your clinic work."

"Back off, Penny."

"It's not hard to guess. You didn't see her for counseling at church, so it had to be the center. And . . . "

"Stop right there. You're into something you have no right to." She was inches away from the truth. She'd probably guessed it already, and that was dangerous.

"But I . . . "

"Not a word! You start speculating and people could be hurt." He raised his hand as he had done in his sermon that morning. "Not another word — to anybody."

"Have I ever betrayed you?" she cried.

He wrapped his arms around her and held her close. "No," he said. "Never."

Eleven

The Women's Health Center compiled a weekly report that was sent on to the main office in Los Angeles. It was nothing more than statistical information listing prescriptions issued, procedures performed, tests taken and their results; no personal data, just figures that wouldn't mean anything to anyone except those by whom and for whom the reports were made.

Rich absentmindedly perused the columns of numbers as he sipped his coffee his second Monday on the job. His eyes caught something questionable. Only one of the women seen that week had opted to carry her child to term. That was his Mrs. Jones. Virginia Miller.

Women came to the clinic for a variety of services. The center employed two full-time counselors who dealt with a spectrum of problems. Rich realized that volunteer services merely eased the burden of the professionals employed there, and that his experience was far from typical of the things they saw every day. But he had counseled only half the abortion candidates. What had happened to the other half, and why had so many chosen to destroy their babies? If they were truly shown every option, wouldn't there be more than five percent who would choose to let their babies live? Rich determined to look farther into it.

He checked past reports still on file; he talked casually to the clerical personnel who made up the reports. He learned that the philosophical bent of the counselor seen had a great bearing on whether the woman kept her baby or not. That was logical, Rich supposed, but grievous, too. He _could_ be an influence. Mrs. Jones was _not_ a fluke. He shuddered to think what might have happened had she seen one of the overworked professionals. He had met them both; they were good people and wouldn't encourage a patient to do something deleterious. But in their rush to meet their day's work schedule, would they have listened carefully enough? Probably yes, most of the time. But what about the exception?

When Rich picked up the work schedule on his way out, he signed up to work all day Monday for the next two weeks. The others would not object; they were happy to have him take all he could handle. It pleased him that the patients they chose to give him were abortion candidates. The issue was still interpreted as a moral one. Who better to counsel women considering the procedure than someone trained to deal with issues of conscience?

A light snow had begun to fall by early evening. The woman in the florist shop on the corner was putting red paper hearts in her display window. She waved at Rich as he passed her. Rich made a mental note to stop there tomorrow and order flowers for Penny.

At home Penny met Rich at the door. "Harry Miller is waiting for you," she said.

"Here?"

"Yes. He's in the living room. I tried to tell him I didn't know when you'd be home and maybe he should come back some other time, but he insisted on waiting."

"It's okay, Penny. I'll handle it."

Harry sat glowering under a child's valentine.

"Hello, Harry." Rich smiled, offering the man his hand.

He didn't take Rich's extended hand. "Can we talk privately?" he asked.

"Certainly." Rich directed Harry to the tiny office at the end of the hall.

When they were seated, Rich asked, "What can I do for you?"

"You can persuade my wife away from the insanity she's chosen."

"What insanity might that be?"

"You know what I'm talking about, and I hold you responsible for it."

Rich smiled inwardly. "It appears to me, Mr. Miller, that you had far more to do with it than I."

Miller looked first shocked, then flustered. His cheeks reddened. "You know what I mean."

"Yes, I believe I do." He leaned back in his chair and folded his hands in his lap while he thought momentarily. "You know, Harry, I've been trained as a counselor; in fact, that's basically my job. It's not an avocation. I've researched abortion from procedure to side effects, and —"

"Don't give me the speech about the procedure causing an emotional strain on my wife. I've heard it, and that's none of your business."

"I believe it is. The clinic uses my services because the law says they have to, and the law was instituted to protect—"

"Can it, Callahan. The only law I'm interested in is the one that says it's legal. We don't want this baby. We're too old to raise another child and that's the end of it."

"Abraham was a hundred . . . "

"Abraham's a myth."

"I see. Perhaps that view ought to be explored the next time church board officers are up for reappointment."

"Don't threaten me!" Harry thrust out his chin belligerently and narrowed his eyes. He stood abruptly and strode toward the door, then stopped. He raised his clenched fist to his chest. "I have the power to break you!"

"I think we both need to calm ourselves," Rich responded. "The question you raised was whether I might be willing to talk with your wife about her pregnancy." Rich weighed his words carefully. "I've already told her I'd talk with her anytime." He opened the top drawer of his desk and removed an appointment calendar. "If you'd like to make an appointment, I'd—"

"I want you to tell her to abort the pregnancy."

"I can't do that." He closed the calendar with a snap.

"Then you'll suffer." Harry stormed through the front of the house and outside. "Hearts and flowers to you, too," Rich mumbled after him.

He walked meekly into the kitchen. "I suppose you heard most of that," he said to Penny as she prepared tuna casserole.

"Yes. Maybe we should send him a valentine."

Rich looked closely at her. She had tears in her eyes.

"I'm sorry, honey."

"No. I'm sorry. I'd guessed what Mrs. Miller was hinting about at church yesterday. But I didn't realize how far it'd gone." She sniffled and grabbed a paper towel to wipe her face. "I don't suppose we'll be here much longer, but you're right. You can't back down."

Rich put his right arm around her shoulders. Penny dropped her spoon in the sink and turned toward him, folding her arms against his chest and snuggling into his embrace. She pressed her damp face against his shoulder and wept. "This was just beginning to feel like home."

"It's not hopeless, Penny. Harry has no real devotion to the church. But he's the chief real estate broker in town. His place on the church's board is important to him. He'd be hurt more than I if all this came out."

"But he knows you won't tell no matter how hard he pushes."

"Yes, and in the meantime his wife will have her baby, and his vindictiveness toward me will have gotten him nothing."

"Nothing but vengeance."

"I don't think he's that sort."

"Then it's over?"

"Yes. I think so." He felt a frown crease his brow. When Penny looked up at him, he forced a smile and kissed her forehead. "Have a nice Valentine's Day."

_____ *Twelve*

Cybil felt a little like the dust bowl refugees she'd seen occasionally in movies, those people who travelled in dust-drenched Model T's loaded down with everything in the world they owned. She laughed as she noted that her brand new red Camaro hardly compared to a dilapidated Model T; and she wasn't on her way to California for a fresh start in life. College was a new beginning, but Chamberlain State was a long way from California. She did have just about everything she owned packed into the car, however; she could barely see through her rearview mirror, and she felt hemmed in on all sides. It all looked so tacky—not the impression she'd hoped to make on her first day of college.

Cybil had become tall and slender; an auburn-haired beauty, she'd tell herself, if it weren't for the freckles that covered her body. She really did feel like a hick — considerably less than chic, anyway — and she felt a little unsure of herself as she drove through Chamberlain on her way toward the campus. She felt relieved to finally pull into the dorm parking lot.

"Hi, Cybil," Julie called as she hurried to her friend's side the minute Cybil stopped the Camaro. Cybil stretched and pulled wrinkled clothing away from her cramped body.

"I've been watching for you from the dorm window," Julie continued. "Wow, girl, the car's as great as you said. I knew it was you the minute I saw you turn off the highway toward the dorms."

Cybil's high school friend and now college roommate walked around the car and eyed it from every angle. "How'd you talk your parents into this one?" she asked when she finally stood next to Cybil again.

"It wasn't so hard — a few tears, a little pouting, and then hugs and kisses at just the right moment — my dad caves in every time! Mom doesn't like it, but she goes along with whatever Daddy wants."

"But you told me before, your mom said no to a car for school."

"Yeah, and she held out all summer. It was 'no' at graduation, 'no' at my birthday in July. I figured that was my last chance. Then yesterday, after you'd already left for here with your parents, my dad drives up to the front of the house with this beauty and hands me the keys. I'll tell ya, Julie, I could've died! It *is* great, isn't it? We are going to have such a great time this year; wheels, and . . . " Cybil searched the side pocket in her shoulder bag, and in a few seconds produced a gasoline credit card, "all the gas we need. Is that too much or what?"

"I don't know, girl. Not too much for me. I'd say it's just about enough," Julie finished, giggling wickedly.

Julie pulled the top two bags off the load in the back seat and said, "C'mon, let's get you moved in. You've got to meet all the kids."

Plenderman Hall was one of the older buildings at the northwest corner of campus next to Chamberlain's main highway. Beyond the campus living complex, endless stretches of farmland lay fallow, waiting for the planting of winter wheat. Ample lawns surrounded the dorms, and the bright yellow plumage of goldenrod, the state flower, filled every flower bed.

The earthy red bricks of Plenderman and Helmsley Halls set them apart from the newer stuccoed buildings nearby. They had been built in the 1950s when college dorms were still designated men's or women's. Cybil and Julie had the choice of the all-women's housing or one of the new coeducational dorms. Cybil would have opted for coeducational living and knew she could've convinced her parents, but Julie's parents were adamant about their daughter staying in Plenderman, so Cybil complied to be with Julie. The bedrooms were arranged in two rows along the outside walls of the building. The bathrooms and laundry facilities on each floor extended down the middle of the building between the rows of rooms. The two girls were assigned a room near the elevator on the fourth floor.

Cybil's room was sparsely furnished and uninviting. She detected a faint smell of disinfectant coming from the restroom across the hall. Julie had livened her half of the room with brightly colored posters and stuffed animals brought from home. Cybil felt encouraged by that reminder of the possibilities. She put the box she was carrying down on her desk, took a poster of a rock group from it, and tacked it up on the bulletin board that hung in front of her. *That helps*, she thought. Her own comforter and pillow would add a touch of home, too. It would be okay.

All the dormitory occupants ate in a common cafeteria at the center of the living complex. It was lunchtime, and Julie held the door open for Cybil as she entered for the first time. The two shorter walls of the large room were almost totally glass. The food service counters occupied a third wall, and a large mosaic mural depicting the harvest covered the fourth wall opposite it. Students dressed in white aprons and paper caps stood behind the counter and replaced food as it was taken. A large, muscular boy wheeled a cart from behind a double swinging door and deposited clean plates, silverware, and trays in the stainless steel display bins at the front of the line. The noise he created, combined with the talk and laughter that filled the room, made

Cybil stop her conversation with Julie and wait until he was gone.

"Is it always this noisy?" she asked as she nervously fingered her plastic-coated meal ticket.

"I don't know; I guess I'm used to it already."

"Where're all the upper class guys?" Cybil asked as she looked around the room and noted that less than a third were men, and most of them looked as if they didn't even shave.

"I wondered about that, too. A lot of the older guys live in frat houses in town—the really good-looking ones, anyway. Those that don't, live in apartments. Getting acquainted isn't going to be as hard as it sounds, though. I'm told that as soon as registration is over the frats all throw parties for the women's dorms just so they can get to know us."

"Look us over, you mean."

"Yeah, so what? We'll both pass inspection. What do we care?"

"Right, I suppose."

Cybil picked up a plastic tray and utensils, set them on the rack at the end of the long food counter, and began drawing herself a glass of milk from the machine in front of her. "Nonfat, 60 calories," she read above the spigot. "What *is* this?"

"Isn't that cute? I guess the nutritionist, everyone calls her Harriet, is a real calorie-counting nut. All the food is marked like that."

Cybil leaned forward and looked up the line. Little white plastic tags with bright red numbers on them stood upright in front of each food selection. "That's *real* cute."

"Anyway," Julie continued, "as soon as you phoned yesterday and said you had your car, I started asking around, and guess what?"

"Dare I ask? What?"

"I've got a couple of upper-class girls from the dorm who are going to take us on a tour of the frat houses."

"What? Are you crazy?"

"No. Isn't that what we're here for—men without parental interference?"

"Sure, but that's a little obvious, isn't it?" Cybil put her tray down at an empty table and sat down behind it. She took a second look at the lasagna she'd selected. It had the tinny smell of canned tomatoes and dehydrated cheese. She took a second sniff as she folded her napkin across her lap.

"We're not going to go in or anything; just drive by, stop and say hello if anyone's outside, that kind of thing. C'mon, Cybil, say you'll do it. It'll be fun."

"All right, I guess. Say, do they ever use fresh ingredients at this place?"

"I should have warned you not to take the lasagna. Harriet's not good at pasta dishes."

"You seem to know a lot for having lived here one day."

"Word gets around. The older girls are only too ready to complain about Harriet's cooking."

"So when are we going on this frat excursion?"

"Today. After lunch."

"What? Thanks for letting me in on it."

"I knew you'd go for it, girl. Are we friends or what?"

"Right, friends."

"How many fraternity houses are there, anyway?" Cybil wiped perspiration from her face. "I've about had it."

"We've saved the best for last. You can't quit now," said Cheryl, a blond junior from upstate who was a Plenderman Hall neighbor.

"I'm with her, Cheryl. It's too hot to be riding around with the windows down and no air conditioning. I'm a wet rag back here," said Tina, a dark-haired girl with braces who was Cheryl's roommate.

"Okay, we'll skip Beta Chi, but we've got to drive by the Alpha Gamms' house."

"Oh, that's a great name," said Cybil. "What's it mean?"

"Alpha Gamma Rho . . . turn right up here," Cheryl directed.

"AGR. Hey, these aren't *ag* boys, are they?"

"Don't let the farm-boy image fool you," Cheryl defended. "This is an ag college, remember. Most of the guys here are ag majors, and the Alpha Gamms are the best. Now turn left, and it's the second house on the left."

The narrow curbless streets made Cybil laugh. *Not exactly uptown*, had been her first reaction. She laughed at herself as she remembered her lack of self-confidence when arriving in her new, overloaded Camaro. But after touring the little college town, she felt rather fond of its quaintness. Most of the houses on this street, like the others they'd seen, were large and old-fashioned with impressive porches that often extended the full width of the house. Windows into the cellars were clearly visible above the ground, and the porches were several steps up from the front yards, giving the homes a substantial look that was absent among the suburban dwellings she was used to. The AGR house looked more prosperous than the other frat houses they'd seen. A young man worked at painting the eaves under the front porch overhang. He stopped his work and whistled loudly as Cybil turned left into their driveway.

"C'mon, let's get out," Julie said as a couple of boys stepped out onto the front porch.

"Just drive by, you said, remember?"

"C'mon, Cybil. It's hot back here; let us out for some air."

"Right," Cybil said, and she opened her door and stepped out. There was a breeze blowing in spite of the warm temperatures, and Cybil admitted that it felt good to get out of the car. The minute they emerged from the car, the yard was filled with young men.

Cybil looked around as she straightened her shorts and smoothed her hair. The guys were all good-looking. They had to be the best of them, as Cheryl had said. *Alpha Gamma Rho,* Cybil thought, *I'll remember that.*

Laundry, room inspections, and doing for herself were all new experiences for Cybil. Her mother had taught her in theory how to take care of herself, but she'd never been forced to do it before. The first month of dorm life was rough. Her dirty laundry grew in the corners of her closet—piles of unwashed blouses and slips blossomed under the bed until finally she ran out of underwear. Then she had to wait in line for the machines. By the time her clothes were clean and dry she'd missed a class or a dorm meeting, and then she was in trouble.

"Where was Val going in such a huff?" Julie asked as she dropped her books on her bed. "She just about knocked me down coming out of here."

"She brought my clean clothes down from the laundry

room." Cybil opened the top drawer of her dresser and began tossing pieces of clothing into it as she folded them.

"Oh-oh." Julie rolled her eyes heavenward in sarcastic disgust. "I keep telling you to rip off the nametags your mother sewed on all your clothes. If they don't know who to blame, you're not in trouble."

"I'd get blamed for *all* the clothes that get left there. For two pins I'd go home." She slammed the drawer closed and opened the next one.

"Quit school? You can't do that! Not now when it's finally getting interesting." Julie fluttered her eyelashes, then winked seductively.

"What do you mean?" Cybil stopped folding clothes and watched her.

"You ought to read the bulletin board downstairs, Cybil; there are some very interesting things posted down there." Julie pulled books and papers from her backpack and plopped them onto her desktop.

"What are you talking about?" Cybil dumped the socks at the bottom of the basket into her top drawer without matching them.

"Alpha Gamma Rho, that's all."

"What?"

"Remember those gorgeous guys we met the first day you were here?" Julie rifled through loose pages of note paper, tossing one after another in the wastebasket by her bed.

"What about them?"

"Our floor's been invited to their first party of the year, this weekend— Friday night! Say, have you seen my anthro notes? I can't believe I lost them."

"Tomorrow you'll be looking for those you're throwing away. Why are your notes loose like that, anyway?"

"Don't nag. And don't change the subject. What do you think of the frat party?"

"It'll be a meat market, not a party."

"Sure. But we'll pass inspection, so what do we care?"

"Can you see Cindy Kellerman at that party?" Cybil picked up her math book and a lap board, arranged some pillows behind her, and sat back against the wall at the head of her bed.

"What a hoot that would be, but that's not our problem."

"No, I suppose not. I just wish there were a better way to meet people."

"You're just feeling down. I promise you, after this party you won't want to go home."

"Hi, I'm Mike Sender," he said once Cybil was in his arms and they were dancing.

She knew who he was. She had noticed him when she first arrived at the party. He was standing near the kitchen door issuing orders to the new fraternity men. Then he turned back into the room, and Cybil thought he had the most dazzling smile. He wore a red large print shirt with the collar turned up, slacks pleated at the waist, full around the hips, and narrow at the ankles. His jacket was a coarse-weave fabric in a dark gray, and the sleeves were pushed up to just below his elbows. His dark hair was slicked back; a few stray locks fell casually down over his forehead just above his left eyebrow.

"And you're Cybil Renwick," he whispered in her ear. They were dancing in the fraternity's large living room. The hardwood floor was duller in the center, from which a roomsize rug had been rolled up and removed. The three-man combo that stood tightly in a corner was playing a slow tune, and Mike pulled Cybil close to him, his right hand pressed firmly against the middle of her back. His embrace warmed her, and she slid her left arm from his shoulder around the back of his neck.

"How did you know?" she shouted to be heard over the sound of the electric guitar.

"I asked. Everyone says the red Camaro belongs to you." Mike waltzed her toward the back of the living room where there was less noise.

"Oh, I get it now . . . " she said more quietly.

Mike laughed. "No, you don't. I have my own wheels. If I weren't interested, the car wouldn't make any difference. You going with anyone?"

"Would I be here if I were?"

He stepped back and looked at her. "You might."

Cybil took mock offense and tried to push herself away.

Mike laughed again and tightened his hold around her waist. "Then you are," he said.

"Going with anyone? No," she said, enchanted by his smile, by the sweet smell of his aftershave, by his even, white teeth.

"Good. How about going to the game with me next weekend? We'll go with a few of the guys here and get something to eat after." Cybil's pulse raced and her heart pounded until she wondered if he could hear it.

"I'd like that," she said coolly.

"Mike Sender? No fooling!" Cheryl said, stretching out on Cybil's bed.

"Why did you say it like that?" Cybil asked as she hooked a heavy gold chain just below her waist, then pulled her knit top up around her middle so that it draped loosely.

"You know how I said the Alpha Gamms were the best frat on campus?"

"Yeah, so?"

"So, Mike Sender's the best of the best."

"That's your opinion," chimed in Tina, thumbing through Cybil's latest issue of *Elle*.

"Mine and that of at least half the female population of Chamberlain State."

"That's debatable."

"Have you ever dated him?" Cybil asked, ignoring Tina. She pulled her long auburn hair forward and brushed the ends, then stood again and let her hair fall naturally back over her shoulders.

"Once. Once or twice is about all any girls gets from him. He's a real grind—doesn't want to be tied down."

"He's dated a few girls more times than that," Tina argued.

"Darn few."

"Uh-huh! I think I've got it. What do I have to do to get a second date with this guy?" Cybil asked, rummaging under her bed for her high-top sneakers.

"No. He's not like *that*. He doesn't expect that from a girl. He's really kind of nice, even square. But if I were you, I wouldn't count on a second date. Enjoy what you've got and forget it."

"Cybil Renwick." Her name crackled over the intercom in her room.

Cybil finished tying the lace on her shoe and jumped up to answer it. She pushed the button under the speaker box. "Yes?"

"Your date's here."

"Thanks. Tell him I'll be right down."

Thirteen

Mike swerved to the right to avoid hitting a blue Toyota pickup that came squealing out of the Plenderman parking lot as they were about to enter it. He and Cybil watched it race up the street toward the highway.

"Hey, we ought to find out what party they're going to! They're sure in a hurry to get there," Cybil said.

"Nah, I know those guys. We can live without their good time," Mike replied.

"Well, I had a terrific time," Cybil said as Mike pulled his car into the nearest parking space. She thought, _I've got to get him to ask me out again. How?_

"We'll have to do it again sometime."

"I've been told not to expect a second date from you," she said.

Mike raised his eyebrows in surprise. He turned the engine off and slipped the keys into his pants pocket. His brown eyes looked directly into hers. "Is that so?" he asked.

He opened his car door and stepped out.

Darn it! Cybil thought, watching his door close behind him, _I didn't play that right._ She had her door open when he approached it from the other side.

"I'm not interested in commitments right now, even temporary ones," he said. "But I do date the same girl more than once."

He braced the door open with his right hand and offered her his left as she stood between him and the car door. The space was tight, and she was delighted that it pleased him.

"That's good news, anyway," she said, her mouth turned down in an appealing pout. "I guess there's hope for me, then." Crickets in the flower beds chirped noisily. A light rain began to fall. The tiny drops caressed Cybil's forehead and cheeks, then mingled to run like tears down her chin. Mike touched one of the little streams and wiped it away with his thumb.

He laughed, then looked away.

"Yes," he said. "I guess there's hope for you." Then he shook his head and laughed again. "I can't believe I said that. You know, I'm really not that stuck on myself. It's just that I'm here to study and . . ."

"You don't need to explain." She leaned close to him and kissed him tenderly. "You don't want any commitments."

Without taking his eyes from hers, Mike wrapped his arm around her shoulders and drew her to him. He returned her kiss.

"Ummm," she said as they finally parted. "I think it's time for me to go in."

The mist diffused the glow of his headlights, creating the illusion of one big beam, as he pulled away from the curb.

"How'd it go?" Julie asked the minute Cybil walked through their door. She eyed the clock whirring in an electric silence on the bookshelf. Eleven fifty-seven. "You almost missed curfew. And look what you did miss!"

Cybil stood staring at an enormous stuffed teddy bear that occupied the major portion of the floor between Julie's bed and her desk. It wore a white sweatshirt with a red *U* on the front.

"Where on earth . . . hey, that's State U's mascot . . . isn't it?" Cybil looked more carefully at the nearly six-foot-high beast smiling cheerfully back at her.

"Shhh." Julie closed the door behind Cybil.

"C'mon, Julie. Get that thing out of here. What're you doing with it, anyway?"

"You're not the only one who had a good time tonight." Julie giggled with excitement. "Cheryl and I and a couple of girls from the second floor met these Delta Sigs after the game and were on our way to a party with them when we passed by old Banger Bear just sitting there all by himself. We couldn't believe it! It turned out that the ones who were supposed to take care of him got tired of carrying him and left him to get their car and come back and pick him up. The game was long over and the field was pretty well deserted. I guess they figured he was safe. Anyway, there were nine of us, and one of our guys had one of those little pickups. We each grabbed something to hang onto and ran with him. The pickup was just driving away when the other guys showed up. They saw old Banger in the back of the truck and took out after it. The rest of us came back here. We bought some drinks and chips and were just starting to party when the two guys with the bear showed up."

"You mean the two guys from State U?"

"No. Our guys. Isn't that a scream? They slipped into the alley behind the theater. The others tore up H Street past them. When it was safe they brought the bear here."

"Why do we still have it?"

"Someone's got to hide him. The frat house is the first place they'll look."

"Julie, we're in deep trouble if they find that thing in our room."

"No one's going to find him tonight. Tomorrow morning before dawn, Chet and Philemon—isn't that a scream of a name?—Oh, but he is so-o-o cute . . . "

"Cut with the 'cute' number and get on with it."

"Right. They're coming at 5:00 AM. They'll flash their headlights as a signal. We'll tie this around it," Julie said, producing a length of twine from her desk, "and let it down from our window. Simple, huh?"

"This isn't going to work. We'll all be expelled. We're going to get caught with it and your *friends* won't even know our names!"

"Don't be so square. What's happened to you, anyway? You're the one who always got us into trouble when we were home."

"Cutting classes and climbing into windows after curfew are not the same as stealing."

"It's just a prank, Cybil. No one's going to treat this like a crime."

"I wouldn't be so sure."

"Well, we're not going to get caught."

"I hope not."

At 5:00 AM Julie hovered at the window for the signal. Cybil woke when she heard Julie snap the screen loose and pull it into their room.

"Are they here yet?" Cybil asked in a sleepy whisper, peering into the darkness outside the window.

"I just saw them pull into the parking lot. Darn! It's raining cats and dogs out there . . . "

Julie was about to turn the light on when Cybil stopped her.

"Are you nuts? We don't want to attract any more attention than we have to."

"No one's out there to see . . . "

"How about campus cops, Julie? They roll by here every once in a while, you know."

"Okay. No lights."

Cybil helped tighten the knots around the bear's middle and then pushed him through the open window. The boys in the car flashed their headlights once and pulled parallel to the curb. Cybil prayed silently that the housemother was sound asleep as they lowered the bear past her window on the first floor. When it was on the ground, they tossed the cord out of the window behind it and snapped the screen back into place. The boys crept across the grass, threw a plastic tarp over the bear, and ran to their truck with it. They were out of the parking lot before the girls were back in bed.

"Whew." Julie flopped backward across her bed. "It's over."

"Maybe." Cybil watched the sky brighten into ribbons of pale pink and gold. "If your friends don't get caught."

"Don't be such a wimp, girl. They're not going to get caught. Hey!" She sat up and leaned toward Cybil at the window. "You never told me about your date with Mike."

"Forget it." Cybil turned away from her and climbed back into bed, pulling the covers over her head. "I've got another hour's sleep. We can talk in the morning."

Cybil and Julie were eating their breakfast in the student union when Mike took a seat at their table.

"I guess you've heard all the noise about the State U's bear," he said as he sat down.

Cybil gave Julie a dark look before answering. "We've heard. They don't know who did it, do they?"

"Not yet." Mike grinned mischievously, taking a bite from his stack of pancakes.

"Where did you hear about it?" Julie was wide-eyed with modest innocence.

"There were a couple of Delta Sigs talking big outside on the quad this morning."

"Oh, great. Those mor—" Julie stopped short when she caught Cybil's frown.

Mike smiled and continued. "Somebody apparently brought the thing to the quad this morning in a small pickup truck—a truck like the one that almost did us in when we drove into Plenderman last night."

Julie swallowed hard and looked wide-eyed at Cybil. Cybil remained calm and looked straight at Mike.

"Is that right? There must be a dozen of those trucks on campus," she said.

"That's true, but the guys driving this one were Delta Sigs. I know them."

"Really? That's interesting," Cybil said.

"I got curious and I asked around. That truck had been there for a party after the game. A party you and Cheryl organized," he added, pointing a spoonful of sugar directly at Julie. He dumped it into his coffee and stirred it with deliberation.

Julie blanched and slid down in her seat.

Mike leaned forward and whispered to both girls, "What've you two been up to?"

"It was—" Julie squeaked.

"Nothing," Cybil finished quickly. "None of what you've said adds up to anything."

"It's enough to make the rent-a-cops ask questions."

"Are you going to tell them what you know?" Cybil asked.

Mike laughed and swallowed the last of his coffee.

"No," he finally said. "But this has given me a whole new picture of you," he said, looking at Cybil and still grinning broadly.

"I was with you last night, remember?"

"Until midnight, yes. I figure Julie had the bear in your room when you got up there."

"You think you have this all figured out. Well, I wouldn't have done it, but— "

"But a friend in need is a friend indeed." Mike laughed again. "It won't go any farther. I'm the only one who can connect the Delta Sig's truck to you. The campus police won't figure it out. And even if they do, the farthest it will go is to the frat house. Delta Sigs aren't the best, but even they won't turn you in."

Cybil relaxed and smiled. "Thank goodness," she said under her breath.

Mike laughed. "You know, you shouldn't hang around the kitchen if you can't take the heat."

_____Fourteen

The months had passed slowly after Rich's initial meeting with Harry Miller in February. It was not until September that Rich could say that that trial was truly over. During those months, the cantankerous older man had kept his promise to cause problems for Rich. He'd begun by secretly spreading half-truths about Rich's clinic work among the church's other board members. Rich became aware of this when the other members asked him questions about that work and told him there'd been complaints. He cried inside as he thought of Penny and their new home. He could save himself and explain his position if he were free to tell what he knew about Harry Miller. But that, of course, was unthinkable. He bit his tongue and defended his work as best he could, praying that the board would understand.

"Why don't you just resign from the clinic?" Mrs. Browning asked when Rich told her how anxious he and Penny were to stay in Chamberlain. "It'd solve the whole problem."

"Is there really that big a problem? Is the board being swayed by the rumors about me?" The walls of Rich's spacious office seemed to close in on him. He felt sick, and the artificial heat added a feeling of wooziness.

"I can't speak for the others, Reverend. But the idea of our pastor working in an abortion clinic gives me pause, his motives notwithstanding. It'd be easier if you'd quit the volunteer work and stick to church business."

"It is church business," Rich whispered angrily under his breath.

Mrs. Browning looked stunned.

"I'm sorry. There's nothing more I can say to defend my actions. I feel that my clinic work is consistent with my duties as your pastor and I can't in good conscience quit it."

"That's a mighty courageous pose for someone who wants to keep his job."

Rich felt himself wilt as he sank back against his chair. "Mrs. Browning, I'm no hero and I don't feel courageous at all. But my perception of my *job* here includes dealing with wrongs I see being done in my community. I can't turn my back on evil. If doing my job as I see it means I must ultimately lose it, then so be it."

Rich couldn't tell whether he'd won that discussion with Mrs. Browning or not— nor any of the dozen or so other similar talks he'd had with other board members. He prayed about it constantly and fought to hide his fears from Penny. The rest was up to the Lord.

Finally, at the church's board meeting in March, Harry Miller moved for Rich's dismissal. The sun was shining, but snow still lay in patches on roofs and lawns. It was an ugly time of year, Rich thought, when snow fell less frequently, the leavings turning black with dirt, and when daytime temperatures turned snow to slush which froze to ice during the night. Harry's dismissal proposal seemed to fit the mood of the last few weeks of winter, and Rich sat silently brooding as he waited for the other board members' reactions.

There was a long, painful pause as board members seemed to poll each other's faces for whatever unspoken agreement might be there.

"On what grounds?" Mrs. Browning finally asked.

"You know what grounds, Hazel," Harry answered. "Conflict of interest. He's spending too much time at that women's health center."

"That's not a conflict of interest," Mrs. Browning replied, and the other board members joined in. "It's his own time, Harry," someone said. "He's explained his purpose at the center. I don't see any conflict at all." "I like to see our church leaders involved in community service." "We've heard enough about this over the past several weeks. If there's no second, Madame Chairman, I suggest we go on to more pressing business." "What's your problem, Harry, the reverend's sermons rub you wrong?"

Harry blustered and sat back in his chair. Rich smiled inwardly and silently thanked goodness for honest people.

"You got something you'd like to say about this, Reverend?" quiet Mr. Collins asked from the far end of the table.

"No, I think you've said it all."

The following few months had gone smoothly. Harry glowered at Rich at every meeting, but except for that, Harry pretty well left Rich alone. Rich worked at staying out of the other man's way until on one hot and muggy Sunday in June he thought he noticed a change in Virginia. The baby was due in less than a month, and the humid summer weather had worn thin on her. Rich understood that. But something had happened to the sparkle she'd acquired and maintained since that first meeting. Two more Sundays passed, and at each meeting Virginia Miller's spirits seemed to dip a little lower. By the third week Rich thought he detected signs of real depression. She avoided his eyes as he looked out from the pulpit, and after the meeting he had to make a point to take her hand when he saw her descending the front steps of the church. Otherwise he was certain she'd have left without a word.

"How are things going?" he asked cautiously. When she tried to withdraw her hand, he put his left hand on top of it and pulled her closer.

"I'm fine, Reverend." She wiped at perspiration that gathered in pools at the base of her neck. "It's just the end of my time, and the weather . . . you know."

"There's more, I can see it. Harry's attitude—it hasn't changed?"

"No . . . well, yes, it has, but not for the better."

"What?"

"It's nothing . . . " She turned away, her voice trailing off.

Rich looked around to see Harry waiting impatiently at the curb for his wife to join him. He looked alarmed and angry. He'd taken his suit coat off and thrown it across the back seat of his car, and he stood rolling up the sleeves of his dress shirt as if he were preparing for a fight.

Rich took Virginia's arm and directed her toward the chapel's big double doors. "Let's go inside for a moment and get out of this heat," he said.

Virginia looked back at her husband, who motioned for her to come. "All right," she said in little more than a whisper. "I'd like to talk." She turned and began to climb back up the steps.

"Bobbie," Rich called to his son, who waited nearby. "Go down to the curb and tell Mr. Miller that his wife will be just a minute. Then find your mother and tell her I might be a little late for dinner."

Ushers stood inside the entry to the chapel waiting to close the heavy outer doors. Rich directed Virginia past them into the chapel and up the aisle toward his office. The large room felt cool, and Virginia put her perspiration-soaked handkerchief back in her purse. She walked a little ahead of Rich in that half shuffle, half waddle Rich remembered so well from watching Penny at the end of her pregnancies. But Virginia's shoulders had more slope to them than Penny's, and her arms seemed to hang like weighty pendulums with no life of their own.

"Now, what's happened?" Rich asked once they were in the office and both seated. His chair faced hers. He held her hand and looked into her face as he spoke. She looked away from him.

"Nothing, really. I thought . . . I'd hoped that as my time drew nearer, Harry would warm to the idea of another baby. He's really a very good father, you know." She turned to look at Rich, anguish apparent on her face. "Anyway, his attitude hasn't warmed at all. He's mellowed some, but he's become more distant—indifferent, kind of." She rubbed the back of her neck with tense fingers. "I'm afraid . . . "

"Afraid? You feel threatened?"

"No. I don't mean that. We really shouldn't have this baby if we can't love it, and my love alone isn't going to be enough."

Rich cringed inwardly as he thought of all the messed-up kids he'd seen in counseling whose authoritarian fathers really didn't love them or couldn't show it. She was right. Her love alone wouldn't be enough. A sharp pain of doubt stabbed at him. Had he been wrong to fight Harry and to encourage Harry's wife to oppose him? Would the child have been better off . . . ? No! He felt his soul shout within him. Life is precious, whatever problems it brings with it! It would be Harry's choice to ignore or abuse his child—Rich had no blame in that. That didn't mean no responsibility, however. He'd watch this closely and be there when . . . Rich's thoughts were interrupted when his office door suddenly swung open and bounced against the doorstop on the wall.

"Reverend, haven't you caused enough damage in my household?" Harry stood in the doorway, his hands doubled into fists, his elbows pulled back like a cocked gun ready to go off.

"Calm down, Harry. Virginia and I are just having a little visit. Come in and join us." Rich stood and pulled a chair up close to Virginia's and directed Harry to it.

"No way. We're leaving." He advanced two paces and took his wife's elbow in his large hand.

Rich gently touched Harry's wrist, then wrapped his long, slender fingers around it. He could feel the tension in the big man's grip and wondered why Virginia wasn't wincing with pain.

"Harry, don't be hasty." Rich spoke in a slow, quiet monotone. "I'm your minister as well as your wife's. I'd hoped that meant something to you. I'm not trying to cause trouble between you. I want to help, can't you see that?" Rich felt the lump in his throat the same time Harry apparently heard it. Tears welled up in his eyelids. He wasn't sorry. Harry relaxed his grip and turned to look at him. The two men stood staring at each other for a long moment. Rich broke the silence.

"Please sit down, Harry, and let's talk." He wiped his face quickly with his handkerchief, then pushed it back into his pocket.

Harry sat slowly. He rested his forearms on the arms of the chair and twisted his hands into a double-fisted knot.

Rich remained silent, sitting forward in his chair and staring intently at the other man's tortured face. "What's wrong, Harry?" he finally asked.

Virginia watched nervously, then began to speak. "It's been difficult—"

Rich stopped her with a touch and a smile. "Harry, Virginia's already told me what she's feeling. I'd like to hear your thoughts."

Harry looked up, and Rich detected the first real softness he'd seen in him. His eyes were wide and sad, the brows arching to a point over his nose. "How can I answer that when I don't know what Virginia's told you?"

"This isn't a debate. I'm not asking for a rebuttal. I want to know what you feel. Your wife was just telling me what a good father you are."

Harry looked at his wife for a long moment, then back at Rich.

Rich weighed his words carefully. "She's hoping you'll be the same kind of father to this new child, but she's uncertain about that."

Harry's face hardened and he sat suddenly erect. "Don't patronize me."

Rich sat back in his chair and tightened his fists around the armrests. "Is that how this appears to you?" He felt the anger that built in him. He forced his fists to relax their grip on the chair and folded his hands in his lap. He thought about all that had happened between him and Harry. Then he nodded humbly.

"Yes, I can see that. I'm sorry. The problem is that neither one of us has had a kind word to say to each other in more than six months. How can you trust me to tell you the truth? I guess, Harry, you're just going to have to trust your wife instead. But in order to do that, you have to talk." He looked from Harry to Virginia, then back again; neither one looked up. Virginia clung to the tissue box and stared at her hands, and Harry's head turned toward the door that stood wide open. "I suggest you take your children home and point them toward the peanut butter and jam, then you two try out that new Chinese restaurant on Third Avenue. And talk, Harry, talk to your wife instead of withdrawing. Agreed?"

Harry nodded, stood, and took his wife's arm—more gently this time. Without a word they walked to the open door.

Rich felt dissatisfied with Harry's response. "Harry, the restaurant is a good place to start, because it forces you both to stay civil; but continue the talk at home where you can be alone and *listen* to each other."

Harry directed Virginia through the doorway without responding.

"Harry?" Rich persisted.

Harry patted his wife's shoulder gently, then turned back toward Rich. "Yeah, okay, Reverend. We'll talk—and listen."

The baby was a healthy boy who cried so much the day his parents had him christened that they hadn't brought him back to church since—at least a month. When Rich and Penny visited their home, Harry wasn't there, which meant Rich hadn't seen Harry and Virginia together in all that time. September arrived in blistering heat, announcing the end of summer, and still there was no proof that all was well in the Miller household. That thought nagged at Rich as he tried to put the finishing touches on the sermon he was to deliver in . . . he looked at the clock on the wall and gasped, gathering his papers quickly into their folder and standing simultaneously. People would be arriving soon.

He felt like a thief as he arranged his notes on the podium and returned quickly to his office. The chapel felt cool in spite of outside temperatures in the nineties and humidity that would wilt the bark off a tree. *Thank goodness for air conditioning*, he thought as he draped his robe and vestment around his neck. He'd talk to Harry today, he told himself, and make an appointment to visit in their home. He picked up his Bible as he heard the choir begin to sing.

People continued to file in through the back doors as the congregation sang the opening hymn. It looked like a record crowd. *Probably escaping the heat*, Rich thought, smiling inwardly. *Whatever it takes.*

The congregation sang the last "Amen" and Rich stepped back up to the podium. The back door opened one last time, admitting Virginia Miller carrying a diaper bag and an infant seat, and behind her . . . Harry carrying their son. Their two older children trailed in after them.

Rich stood stunned momentarily, choking back tears. He rubbed his eyes and took a second look. The baby lay awake and content in his father's arms, and Harry smiled sheepishly. But there was nothing sheepish about Virginia's grin. She wrapped her arm under her husband's elbow and winked when she caught Rich's eye. Rich ended his reverie when he noticed the rest of the congregation turning around to see why he was staring.

"Love is the miracle," he began his sermon, pulling attention back to himself. His voice cracked and he cleared his throat, looking again at the family at the back of the room. "*Love* is the miracle . . . "

_____Fifteen

"I'm going home for the weekend, Julie." Cybil took a small suitcase off the shelf in her closet. "Want to come?"

"No. I've got to crack some books. And you do too, girl. Your midterm grades weren't any better than mine. Why are you taking off now, anyway? Your folks'll just do the same thing mine would do — give you a bad time about studying more."

"I can handle my folks," Cybil sighed. "It's this scene I can't handle."

"What? There's a frog who doesn't jump when you command. Which one is it? Phil? Steven?"

"Forget it, Julie." Cybil pulled clothing out of drawers, arranging them quickly into the satchel on the bed.

"Oh, I know. It's the biggest frog in the pond! You ought to be content, you know. Mike goes with you more than he goes with anyone else. Isn't that enough?"

Cybil stopped and looked straight ahead for a moment. Then she turned suddenly and threw herself into the armchair next to her desk. Fall had hit Nebraska with a flurry of rain, sleet, and driving winds. Cybil hadn't felt warm in days, and today was no exception.

"No, it's not enough. I really like him — a lot."

"So? I'm sure he likes you — a lot."

"Me and twelve other girls." Cybil reached out with her toe and pushed at a pair of rolled-up socks that had fallen onto the floor in front of her. Her lower lip quivered and she bit it hard. "I just saw him downstairs with Sandy Hendleman. He had the nerve to wave, like it's all okay or something."

"Cybil, you date a half dozen different boys and don't try to hide it from any of them. You'd rather Mike sneaked around?"

"No." Cybil felt her lip protrude again. She knew her brooding over his dating other girls was irrational, but that didn't change her feelings. "I've just got to get out of here, that's all." She jumped up and hurried through the rest of her packing.

"You know, girl, you have the formula for keeping Mike glued to you if you want to use it."

Cybil stopped short. "Bed and breakfast? Forget it, I can't go that far."

"Maybe you won't have to go that far. 'A few tears, a little pouting, and then hugs and kisses at just the right moment.' It works on your dad, doesn't it?"

"What are you talking about?"

"Mike's a man, isn't he? I mean, he isn't as old as your dad, but I can't see what difference that makes."

"Julie, you've got to be kidding. I can't work Mike the way I work my dad."

"Sure you can! You do it all the time. You're an artist! I'll bet it'll work."

Cybil stood still, suitcase in hand, and stared at Julie. After a few seconds she looked away, then shook her head and grabbed her purse. "No. I couldn't do that. It wouldn't work on Mike. I'm leaving; I'll be back Sunday night. See you then."

Cybil cracked her window and endured the cold in order to enjoy the freshness of the air. As she sped down the long straight highway her mind wandered. *Mike's a man, isn't he?* she heard

Julie repeat. *You do it all the time. You're an artist!* She'd certainly learned over the years how to manipulate her dad. It was second nature to her now. She had come to know she could have anything she wanted from him.

When she thought about it at all, she realized she hated her father for his weakness. "No, no," she said out loud, "I don't hate him." Her temples throbbed as she thought about all the times she'd maneuvered him into saying *yes* when she'd wished he'd say no. When he didn't, she *did* hate him—for the moment, at least. But she loved him, too. She loved the things he did for her. She'd made his life miserable over the things she wanted most. And yet a part of her wanted him to say no more than anything.

She wanted Mike. She wanted him as much as she had ever wanted anything. But badly enough to manipulate him as she did her father? Was it worth the price?

"Your father won't be home until Monday night, maybe Tuesday," Cybil's mother said. The girl struggled to keep her disappointment from showing. "Something wrong? You can call him and talk on the phone."

"I could've done that from school."

"Then there is something wrong." Her mother laid aside her needlepoint.

Cybil looked away, then smiled. "Not really. I wanted a man's point of view on something."

"Can I help?"

"No, thanks." Cybil could see the hurt in her mother's eyes. She hadn't intended that, but she didn't want her mother's advice. She knew what it would be. "Go back to school and forget about boys! You're there to study and get good grades," she'd say. "There'll be time for the other later"—and on it would go.

It was ironic that her mother's advice would be the same as Mike's. "Let's keep this casual," he'd said to her recently. She'd agreed, but only to please him. Julie was right, she did maneuver Mike in a way—subtly. But she never made direct demands on him, as she did with her father. Her father was a captive audience, after all—she couldn't lose him. Mike could be pushed away, and that would be unthinkable. If she were more certain of his feelings for her, she might use those against him, but if he didn't care that much, her strategy would backfire.

Cybil spent the rest of Saturday and all morning Sunday brooding. By noon Sunday she was packed and ready to start back to school. She dressed in the Levi's and giant-sized shirt she'd saved for the trip back and went out to the enclosed porch that bordered the back edge of the house. It was warmer on the porch than it was outside, but the thermometer still wavered at fifty degrees. She slumped down onto the platform swing and wrapped an old afghan around her.

"Cybil?" She heard her mother call from the front of the house.

Cybil pulled the crocheted blanket up tighter around her and sank down further into the soft cushions of the ancient swing. She tightened every muscle in her body for a moment, then relaxed with a sigh and answered.

"I'm out here, Mom."

The cat she had loved as a child had died. The one kitten they had kept from the last litter was now the family's only pet, and she jumped into Cybil's lap just as Mrs. Renwick stepped out onto the porch.

"Sassy," Cybil murmured sweetly as the cat rubbed its graceful body against her afghan-covered arms. There had been a succession of "Sassys" over the years, each new Sassy comfortably wearing the familiar name. Cybil took the animal and rewrapped the blanket around them both. "*You* love me, don't you?" She rubbed the furry creature against her cheek.

"Of course she does," her mother snapped, holding the screen door at bay, half inside and half out, on the porch. Her face was pinched and troubled.

"I was just kidding, Mother. Don't look so glum."

Marianne Renwick took a quick breath and stood suddenly erect, shivering without her sweater. "Your lunch is ready," she said. "Shall I bring it out here?"

"If you don't mind," Cybil replied, and ached a little at having offended her mother again. She seemed to be very good at that. "And yours, too," she added loudly enough to be heard from the kitchen.

Cybil set the cat down on the porch floor when her mother reappeared from the kitchen with a small tray of steaming tomato soup and a toasted cheese sandwich.

"It's too cold out here for me," Mrs. Renwick said as she set the tray on her daughter's lap. "I'll eat in the kitchen."

"Then I'll come inside with you."

"No, don't bother."

"Mother! Don't do this to me. I want to have my lunch with you." Cybil held the lunch tray carefully above her head with one hand as she unwrapped the blanket from around her with the other. She followed her mother into the kitchen. They sat across the table from each other and began to eat. Cybil endured the silence for several minutes and then spoke.

"It's been kind of quiet here without Dad," she began. "But I've enjoyed the weekend. It's nice to spend time with you, Mother," she added stiffly.

"It's been nice for me, too."

They were silent again.

"I'm going to work a little harder on my grades. I'm sure you and Dad were disappointed in my midterms."

"I'd say you need to work a *lot* harder."

Cybil looked straight at her mother, but Marianne didn't look up from her lunch plate.

"I'll try. I'm sorry," she sighed.

She pushed her chair away from the table and took her dishes to the sink. "I guess I'd better go. I want to be back before dark." She put on her coat and picked up her purse and satchel and turned to leave when her mother stopped her.

"Hug and a kiss?" her mother said. It was a phrase Cybil had heard her mother use many times before — practically every day of her life as she had gone off to school. She kissed her mother's cheek and hugged her tightly.

"I'll have your father call you as soon as he gets in," her mother said.

"Thanks."

Sixteen

"That was a great lunch," Cybil said as she and Mike gathered up the picnic things and loaded them back into the box. "Homemade pita stuffed with crab, shrimp, sprouts, and that wonderful sauce — and the cake, too. You didn't make all that yourself, did you?"

"My housemother likes me," Mike replied, taking her hand and stroking her long, delicate fingers.

"You're telling me she did this just for you?"

"She's a sweetheart. What can I say?" he squeezed her hands gently and let them go.

"I'm jealous."

"Of her, you have a right. Of course, she's sixty-three, and by the time I graduate . . . "

"Okay, okay." Cybil threw a paper napkin at him.

"You know, Cybil, you don't need to worry about the other girls I date."

"Where did that come from? Do I look worried?"

"Just a hunch I have."

"You don't worry about me, and I won't worry about you." A knot she couldn't swallow began to grow in her throat. She rose, her back to him.

Mike watched her carefully as she took their empty bottles and rumpled napkins to a nearby can and then returned to sit beside him.

"I think you do worry," he said, touching her cheek lightly with his fingertips.

Cybil swallowed hard.

"Then why do you date other girls?"

Mike lay back onto the picnic blanket for a moment. Then he turned suddenly onto his side and spoke directly to her. "I told you before, school's all I can handle right now. You know I'm here on scholarship. If my grades drop a single point I lose it and I'm out of here. And I'm just barely making it."

"What's that got to do with me and dating?"

"I've seen the guys who have steadies. Pleasing their girl gets to be the most important thing in their lives."

"So? That sounds nice to me."

"If I have studying to do or a paper to write, I stay home and do it regardless of what else is going on."

"And?"

"Cybil! I miss homecomings, championship games, spring formals, even frat parties, if I have work to do. That means you'd miss those things, too. And don't try to tell me you wouldn't put pressure on me to take you. If I were the only guy you were dating, you'd put the pressure on. As it is I have total control, and that's how it has to be."

The temperature had turned suddenly colder as the sun dropped into a cloud bank. The white sky turned crimson. Cybil stood and brushed her pants off. The ground was damp, and even the heavy blanket Mike had provided had not kept moisture from absorbing into her clothing. She smoothed the wrinkles along her legs and pulled her coat more tightly around her.

"I guess a picnic in November was a poor choice." Mike pulled himself up, picked up the blanket, folded it, and tucked it under his left arm. Together they walked down to a small lake that had partially thawed in the recent unseasonably warm weather.

"Don't apologize. It was fun, and it's the only time of year we'd have this park to ourselves. It was a beautiful day—almost like spring."

"If it were any colder the lake would be busy with skaters," Mike commented.

They sat together on one of a string of benches that rimmed the lake's circumference. Mike put his arm around Cybil's shoulder and kissed her tenderly on the side of her face. She turned toward him and they kissed—simply at first, and then passionately. Cybil felt Mike's arms tighten around her, and she enjoyed their closeness. After several breathless minutes, he released her and backed away. Cybil saw Mike's hands tighten into fists inside his coat pockets. The muscles in his face were tense, and he stared blindly at some distant spot. She was glad she'd affected him so, but she knew that the tension only added to his resolve. She'd seen it before. He'd start dating other girls again and wouldn't be back to her for a long while.

She stood and slowly walked around behind him. There were still pockets of snow where the bench shaded it from the sun. She took a handful and began molding it. It crunched in her fingers. He turned and looked up at her. "What are you up to?"

"Oh . . . nothing . . . much," she giggled as she grabbed his collar and shoved the icy snow down the back of his neck, then turned and ran. He stood, bent in half, and brushed at the snow that clung to his neck and shirt. Then he grabbed a fistful himself.

"In a mood for games, huh?"

Cybil stopped her flight and turned to face him. The snow in his hands was hard and crusty. He turned the sparkling chunk over and over but couldn't shape it. After a moment he gave up, dropped it to the ground, and began backing toward the lake's edge. There was a small drift nestled in among the roots of an old tree at the water's edge where the slushy ice helped keep it cold and soft.

"Aha!" Cybil shouted as he backed away. She felt fun building in her. She pushed her sweater's hood back until it fell away from her head. The cool air felt good against the back of her neck. "Giving up, Sender?" She looked around where she stood and saw nothing but bare, damp ground. She edged stealthily sideways toward a wooded area where snow still clung to tree limbs.

"Not a chance, Renwick. You started this, I'm going to finish it." Cybil watched him carefully. He grinned broadly as he returned her stare. "And don't think I don't see what you're doing," he said. "I'll nail you before you get to the trees, so you'd just as well stop and take your medicine." He bent quickly, grabbed the snow, cupped it easily in his large hands, and heaved it just as Cybil turned to run for more ammo. His shot hit her squarely against her shoulder and splattered up against her unprotected cheek. It stung momentarily. Some clung to her face and slithered down her neck. She laughed out loud and kept running.

"Hey, no fair, Renwick. The game's got rules. I got you fair and square. You're dead."

"Who says I play fair?" She grabbed a fresh supply of bark-encrusted snow and overhanded it. He ducked. She missed. He bent down again, scooped up a large mound of slush, cradled it against his body as if it were a misshapen white football, and ran toward her. She backed away, then turned and ran. "Okay," she screamed. "I concede. You win." She tripped on a dead tree branch in the soft ground and fell.

In two more steps he was even with her. He watched her turn over and begin to scoot backwards away from him. He laughed and dropped to his knees beside her.

"Concede? What? You running for office? The word's 'uncle.' Renwick, say it — 'uncle.' "

"Uncle," she choked out. She was almost breathless with laughter. He reached his free arm around her waist, still hugging the wet snow to his chest with the other.

"Louder, Renwick." He deposited the snow above her shoulder next to her face and pulled her to him. He pinned her body beneath his and reached for two fistsful of snow. She felt his knee between her legs. Her heart raced. "Shout it, Renwick, or I start stuffing this into that pretty little mouth of yours."

"Uncle, uncle," Cybil shouted. She closed her eyes and clenched her teeth together tightly. She felt almost panicky with excitement. Nothing happened, and she opened her eyes. His face was so close that she could feel his breath meet hers, then fan out past both cheeks. She smelled the fresh woodsy fragrance of his aftershave mixed with the heady masculine scent that was all his. He hesitated for only a moment, then pressed his lips to hers. She felt him drop the snow in his hands above her head, then rock her gently sideways until he could get his arms all the way around her. When the kiss came to its natural conclusion, he reached for another, then another. He breathed heavily, and beads of sweat covered his forehead. He kissed her face next to her mouth, then her cheek, her ear, and around to her neck, then down until she felt his lips against the hollow at her throat where her heart pounded shamelessly.

His breath warmed her, and she wrapped her arms around his shoulders. He removed his arms from around her and she rested back on the ground. She opened her eyes and remembered where she was.

"No," she whispered and pushed him gently away.

"Cybil, don't tell me no now." His words were breathless and pleading.

"I won't," she said. "But not here. Let's go back to the car."

"You're a terrific girl."

"I want to be *your* terrific girl."

"That's what this is all about."

"How long have you been sexually active?" The doctor at the student health center peered at her over the top of his rimless eyeglasses.

Cybil felt numb; she hadn't wanted to come here, she was annoyed that they required her to submit to an examination, and she didn't want to answer any personal questions. Why didn't they just give her the contraceptives she came for and let her go?

"Not very long," she said.

"A month, two weeks?"

"Two weeks, I guess. Maybe more. Since before Thanksgiving."

"That's more like three weeks."

"I guess that's right." The chair she sat in squeaked as she shifted. On the wall behind the doctor, traces of colored ink appeared in pieces through a square patch of paint meant to cover it.

"Why didn't you come in sooner?"

"Listen, I don't want to answer any more questions. Please give me what I came for, and—"

"I'm afraid I can't, Miss Renwick." The doctor removed his glasses and pressed stubby fingers against his eyes. Then he put the glasses back on and squinted at the papers in his hand.

"Why? My friends get theirs here, and—"

"The simple fact is that you're already pregnant."

"No," she whispered as she buried her face in her hands. "There must be some mistake—I can't be pregnant," she assured him. "I can't be."

"You can and you are. There's no mistake. You must've suspected," the doctor said.

"I knew it was possible, but these kinds of things don't happen to . . . " She knew how idiotic that sounded and stopped in midsentence. She stood and walked to the other side of the room.

Cybil could feel tears begin to collect along her lower lids. She bit her upper lip and grimaced, but nothing would stop them.

"What do I do now?"

"We don't take care of pregnancies and related problems here," the doctor began. She heard him open his desk drawer and remove something from it. "There's a women's clinic here in town. I suggest you go there," he said.

"For an abortion." She turned abruptly and faced him. She felt suddenly sick and dizzy. *These things don't happen to —*

"For counseling to help you decide what you want to do. They'll explain all your options."

Cybil stepped back to the desk and took a referral card he handed her. She wiped her tears away with the back of her hand. He offered her a tissue from a box on his desk.

"Thank you," she said, almost as an afterthought.

"Miss Renwick."

Cybil stopped at the door.

"Don't wait too long. The sooner you make your decision, the better."

_____Seventeen

"Hey, Jeff, you're late! We're wasting time," one of the guys in the group hollered as Jeff came walking into their makeshift garage/studio.

"Sorry I'm late." Jeff stuffed both hands in his pockets. George was adjusting the stool behind his drums. He looked Jeff's way and frowned. "C'mon, Jeff. Time's tight. Get your gear out."

"I've got to talk to you."

"Yeah? What about?"

Jeff stepped across the tangle of cords strung from the acoustical paneling to the amplifiers. The other guys were busy testing and tuning equipment. The thump and whine of drums and guitar strings drowned out their voices. "Can we go somewhere private?"

George led the way inside the house and closed the door. "Okay, Jeff, what's comin' down?"

"I'm afraid I might have a problem with the recording date."

"You're kidding!" George turned away from him, picked up a pillow from the couch nearby, and jammed his fist into it. "Ah, man . . . "

"I can explain—"

"No you can't, buddy. There's nothing so important that it can't be changed."

"If you'll listen, it'll all—"

"Listen? You listen! Hallaway busted everything getting this studio time for us. It's our one big break, and you're not going to spoil it! We get this demo done and sent to the big guys, we're on our way. Without the demo no one's got ears. You got that?"

"I know that!" Jeff shouted. "I know that."

"Then what's your beef?"

"It's no beef, George. I just put Maggie on a plane to Norfolk."

"You weren't going to do that until next week—after we record our stuff."

"It was scheduled for next week, but . . . listen, I don't know what happened. Timing in these things is crucial, and now's the time."

"Terrific." George threw himself onto the couch. "Why couldn't it wait until next month?"

"You know what we went through to qualify for this program? We cause the least doubt about our desire to have this baby and they dump us and take the next couple on the list." The house was hot and stuffy. One of the guys was fingering a twangy version of "Jolly Old Saint Nicholas" on his guitar. The irony of hot Los Angeles weather and Christmas together struck him. He thought what a relief a week of cold weather would be and wished he'd flown off to Norfolk with Maggie. He wiped his sweating face against his right shoulder. "You know how many painful procedures Maggie has gone through? She wants this baby that badly. I can't say no to her just because we have a *chance* at a recording contract. It means nothing. We've recorded before and gotten nowhere."

"This is *Century Records*, man. It means everything."

"They can't guarantee us a hit anymore than the others could."

"They can bring us a whole lot closer to it."

"Maybe."

George came to his feet and planted himself in front of Jeff. "This time it's more than just a chance." His look was pleading. "It's everything. We can't miss it!"

Jeff turned away. "We'll get studio time again."

"You got a bankroll stashed away somewhere I don't know about?"

"This thing with Maggie is costing us thousands."

"Right! None of us can afford to pay for studio time. We got lucky and found a couple of hours in the middle of the night when all we have to do is pay the technicians. Hallaway isn't going to find that for us again—not in this decade. We got to grab this while it's hot."

"Look, it might still work out."

"I'm listening."

"Maggie checks into a hotel near the medical center today. They start right away. By this time next week they'll know when they need me. I can fly there when I'm needed—a day there and back—36 hours tops. The problem is, it looks like that's most likely to be Sunday. But there's a flight Sunday night that arrives here at midnight. I've already made reservations."

"That's cutting it close."

"I can drive to the studio in two hours, easy."

George frowned, sighing. "Maggie knows how important this is. I can't believe she'd put you in this spot."

Jeff took a deep breath and turned away from his friend. He tried to swallow the anger that rose in him like an ice floe.

"Don't blame Maggie, George," he said quietly, both hands clenched. "If I'd had my way I'd be on that plane with her. She insisted I stay here to work. She's so uptight about this she's about to pop. She's got to get herself from the airport in a strange city, check into a hotel, handle all the stress at the medical center all by herself. There's no one to smile with if it looks good. No one—" Jeff felt his throat tighten and he swallowed hard— "no one, George, to cry with her if it fails. She knows how important this studio time is to us, so don't you—"

"Okay! Okay, ol' buddy. We'll hang in there and hope. Listen, don't tell the other guys about this. I'll handle it when the time comes."

Jeff found a pay phone in the hospital corridor near the waiting room. He dropped a quarter into the slot and dialed the familiar number.

"How's it going?" Jeff asked when he heard George answer the phone.

"We're all set here."

"You explain to the guys where I am?"

"No sweat. I said you'd be back in time. Don't make me a liar. We need you, buddy."

"What can I say, George? I'm sorry. Maggie needs me, too."

"Yeah, I guess she does," he said. "Listen. Good luck with it. I really hope it works out this time."

"Thanks."

Jeff went back to his seat in the waiting room. He flipped through a magazine blindly, then tossed it on the table next to him. He twisted his wedding ring nervously. It had grown big for him in the past several months. He tried it on his right hand and left it there. Was there a limit to what Maggie would endure to have a child? They obviously hadn't found it yet. This was probably their last possibility. They were among a small number of couples who were diagnosed as being infertile, but for whom no medical explanation could be found. With no specific problem diagnosed, there was no medical cure. Nonetheless, they had tried everything possible—drawing at straws. Now Maggie was undergoing yet another surgical procedure. Jeff silently prayed it would be the last.

In vitro fertilization was new, it was iffy—but it had worked for other couples. The papers were full of success stories of "test tube babies" born in England, in Australia, and in the states—why not Maggie and Jeff? Jeff wanted it to work for them as badly as Maggie did, but he didn't want her to suffer anymore . . .

He ran the fingers of both hands back through his hair, tightening every muscle in his body at the same time. In a moment he relaxed and stepped to a nearby drinking fountain and took a drink.

"You're Jeff Perry, aren't you?" he heard from behind him.

He turned to find a petite blond lady waiting there.

"Yes," he replied.

"I thought so. Is Maggie in surgery now?"

"Yes. I'm sorry, I don't remember . . . "

"Oh, we haven't met. My name's Patrice Gallagher. My husband and I are here for the same reason you are. Maggie and I have gotten kind of close through all this. I knew she was scheduled for today. That's why I came down here. Any news?"

"Not yet."

"Do you mind if I wait with you?"

"I could use some company. I'm feeling pretty jumpy."

She laughed. "My husband, Cliff, felt the same way. He's out playing golf this morning. I made him go. He was driving me crazy. It's kind of funny — Maggie kept him company yesterday while I was in there."

"Then you're one up on us." Jeff pointed toward a couch, and they both sat down.

"I've been one step ahead of Maggie from day one."

"Is that so?"

"Yeah. It took. We're on our way. Maggie doesn't know. I'd hoped to tell her before she went in for surgery. Other people's success is encouraging somehow."

"Mr. Perry?" a voice interrupted. Jeff looked up to face a doctor still in wrinkled green sterile clothing. "You may see your wife now," he said.

"How is she?"

"Fine. Hello, Mrs. Gallagher," the doctor said as he led Jeff into the inner maze of hospital corridors and elevators.

"How'd it go?" The bittersweet odor of antiseptics and anesthetics grew and waned as the doctor led him through one polished-tile hallway after another. Jeff had never liked the smell of hospitals. Doctors made him nervous with their probings and proddings and invasions of privacy.

"Beautifully, Mr. Perry. We won't know about the success of the procedure, of course, for several more days, but the surgery went along without a hitch. Your wife's fine. We were able to retrieve four eggs. You were given a specimen jar?"

"Yes." Jeff touched the coat pocket that held the small plastic cup with its snap-tight lid. Their footsteps echoed through the wide hallways.

"Only one of the eggs was mature. We'll need your specimen in a few hours for the mature egg. Then tomorrow we'll get another for . . . "

"Tomorrow?" Jeff questioned.

"Yes. The immature eggs are being incubated now. We don't know how long that will take, but to insure the best possible chance of implantation we need to get as many of the eggs fertilized as possible."

Jeff frowned and came to a halt.

"Do you have a problem with that?" the doctor asked.

"I have to catch a plane tomorrow evening. I was hoping the whole process would be complete by then and I could go home with at least some good news."

"I'm sure you were told implantation won't happen for at least another day after that."

"Yes. I'll be back before then."

"I don't think you need to worry. We should be done with you by tomorrow afternoon." The doctor walked to the doorway, then turned back and motioned to Jeff to join him. "Frankly, Mr. Perry," he whispered, "whether or not we attain fertilization is critical in this process. If it doesn't happen, your wife's going to need some company to share the disappointment."

When the doctor left, Jeff went into Maggie's room. He felt sick, but he forced a smile.

"Alone at last," Maggie said, looking small and lost in the high white bed under the high white ceiling. She smiled back at him.

Jeff leaned over her bed and kissed her. "You're in a good mood."

"Of course. Aren't you? There's no point in being negative."

Jeff felt tightness grip in his chest. "Let's not hope too hard."

"I'm not, really. I just want this so—"

"I know."

"Did you call George?"

"Yes."

"Did you tell him you can be there?"

"Honey, if this isn't complete by the time I have to go, I'm not going to leave."

"You'll be back here by dinnertime Monday. I can handle it on my own until then. Besides, it is going to happen, right on schedule."

Sunday morning when he arrived at the hospital Jeff found Maggie in her room fully dressed. He stopped at the door and watched her. She was beautiful, her dark natural curls brushed back at the temples and pinned with two small combs. Her face looked freshly scrubbed, and she wore very little makeup—just the way he liked it. He watched her finish packing her robe and slippers into a small overnighter. She cleared the night table of tissues and candy wrappers and dropped them in the wastebasket, then pushed it back into the corner. He smiled and stepped toward her.

"Oh, hi." She turned to him and kissed him. He held her slender waist with both hands and lingered over the kiss.

"Thanks," he said. "That was nice."

"You expected something different?"

"No. I just missed you last night."

"You have no idea how much I—" She stopped and looked over his shoulder past him.

Jeff turned to see their doctor standing in the doorway, and wondered how long he'd been there.

After an awkward pause he spoke. "I'm afraid I have good news and bad news," he said.

Maggie remained calmly quiet.

"Bad news first." Jeff took Maggie's hand.

"It's been nearly twenty-four hours, and the mature egg hasn't fertilized. It doesn't look like that's going to happen."

Jeff squeezed his wife's hand. "And the good news?"

"The other three eggs are nearly ready. We need your second specimen. He handed Jeff a jar and turned to leave. He stopped at the door and added, "Without wanting to be too encouraging, I'd like to add that these three eggs were always our best shot. The one failure was predictable. I didn't want to say that yesterday, but I don't want you to be too discouraged, either."

"Thank you," Maggie said. "We know the odds and we're still hopeful."

"Good." He smiled at her. "We'll see you in the lab." The doctor tapped the lid of the jar and smiled again at Jeff.

Jeff frowned at the jar in his hand before he turned to leave.

They sat together in the hall waiting the result of their last "best shot." White-coated orderlies rattled by, pushing steaming carts of aluminum dinner trays. Jeff's stomach rumbled, and he remembered he'd forgotten to eat lunch. He pushed his fingers over the spot as if they might camouflage the sound and the pain he felt at each growl. All he needed now was an ulcer!

Maggie checked the clock on the wall in front of them. "You've got to go or you'll miss your plane."

"Forget the clock. I'd tear it off the wall if I could."

"You can't ignore it."

"I can do what I want."

"Don't, Jeff; the recording is important."

"*This* is important."

Jeff paced to the lab window and looked in.

"I appreciate your wanting to stay, but I can handle this. I can't handle your missing an opportunity because of me."

"Because of you? I have something to do with this, too."

"Of course, but . . ."

"I'll go as soon as the doctor comes back with the latest word—whatever it is."

"You've barely enough time now . . ."

"Don't, Maggie." With that he sat down again and leaned forward, resting his elbows on his knees. Maggie stretched her left arm across his back. She looked at the clock again and shook her head.

"Hello, you two," came a familiar voice.

They looked up to see the Gallaghers standing over them. Cliff was a slight man a little older than Jeff. He held an overnight bag and the couple's two coats. Jeff stood when they were introduced and offered Patrice his chair.

"Oh, no, thanks. I've got to get settled in."

"You're checking in again?" Maggie asked.

"Tomorrow's the big day for us." Patrice waved her crossed fingers jubilantly in front of them.

"We'll be pulling for you."

"And we for you. You're still waiting for word?"

"Yes."

"The waiting's the worst, isn't it? And it just gets more traumatic with each new phase. Especially when we see women go home every day having failed at one step or another."

"Patrice, I don't think they need to hear—" Cliff began.

"I'm sorry, I didn't mean to—"

"That's all right," Maggie responded. "It's all true. We're still very hopeful—nothing anyone says will lessen that."

The lab door opened. Jeff saw a smile creep across Maggie's face as she looked at the doctor squarely. He was radiant. "It's a go," he said.

Jeff wrapped eager arms around Maggie, and they both wept.

"We've got a way to go yet," the doctor said, "but technically you're parents."

The couple parted finally and looked at each other through their tears.

Jeff eagerly shook the doctor's hand and then Cliff's.

"Congratulations," they both said.

All Jeff could say was "thank you," over and over again.

Maggie looked at the clock. "You've got to go," she said, pushing him away.

"You can get to the hotel all right?" He backed down the hall.

"I'll take her," Cliff said. "As soon as Patrice is settled."

"Great. Thanks!" He raced past the closed elevators and down the stairs.

"It's worth an extra fifty to you if you can get me to the airport in fifteen minutes." Jeff threw himself into the first available taxi.

"You got it, mister."

Jeff's head jerked suddenly backwards as the driver blasted his horn, turned into traffic, and floored the accelerator.

Jeff clutched his boarding pass. With no baggage to check, he had only to make it to the boarding area and get on the plane. The gate attendant was closing the latch when Jeff came running in.

"Just in time, sir—another five seconds and I'd have been out of here."

"Thanks," Jeff said breathlessly. "You're a winner."

Eighteen

"I'm pregnant!" Cybil cried. "Now leave me alone."

"Pregnant? How could you be pregnant?"

"Didn't your mother ever give you that little speech about the facts of life, Julie? It goes something like this: When two people—"

"Of course she did. I'm not stupid, Cybil. At least, not as stupid as you. What did you use—anything?"

"Nothing." Cybil's head ached and she was beginning to be uncomfortably nauseous. "Don't lecture me. Okay? Just shut up, or I'll shove this book down your throat. Okay?"

"Okay. But I think—"

"Don't think. Just shut up!"

"Okay. But what—"

"Shut up!"

"Okay!" Julie backed away and sat in the desk chair on her side of the room.

Cybil returned to her studying but found Julie's silence more disturbing than her chatter had been. After several minutes she turned to see her roommate staring gloomily at the larger-than-life Santa on the wall in front of her. The jolly saint's smile seemed to mock her. Cybil grabbed her robe and towel off the hook in her closet and stepped to the door.

"I'm sorry if I hurt your feelings. We'll talk about it later. I'm going to take a shower," she said, pulling the door open and letting it slam loudly behind her.

It was late at night, and those girls who weren't asleep were studying in their rooms. Except for one girl showering in the stall nearest the door, the bathroom was empty. Cybil walked to the other end of the long line of metal doors and stepped through the last one in the back corner. She slipped quickly out of her clothes, letting them drop to the floor of the dressing cubicle, then turned the water on full force.

As she stepped into the shower, hot water pelted her body, bringing tears to her eyes. She stood it momentarily, then turned and relished the feeling. When it started to feel good to her, she turned the cold tap clockwise a notch and gritted her teeth as the stinging stream became instantly hotter. "Ooo!" she said out loud, dancing delicately in a circle until she was used to the temperature again. Again she closed the cold valve tighter, this time backing away from the stream until it reached only her feet. Then she eased herself back under its force. She watched as her skin turned red, then pushed her head under the nozzle. "Ooo!" she said again, running red hands back across her hair and turning her face into the burning rush. Steam filled the cubicle until she could barely see the faucet handles in front of her.

She reached for the cold again but hesitated, then impulsively turned the cold on full force and the hot off. Water that was cold at first quickly turned icy as water from nearly frozen pipes beneath the ground reached her. "Ooo!" she groaned again, this time shivering. Her red skin turned to goose bumps. Her heart pounded loudly, painfully, in her chest, and she gasped for air, still forcing herself to stay put until her body's every cell cried to be released from the torture. When she finally stepped out of the shower, *she* was crying, too. "Why?" she sobbed. "Why?"

Cybil awakened late the next morning, nauseous again. Julie had been asleep when she got back to their room the night before, and Cybil was glad for it. She forced herself out of bed, locking her teeth against the sickness rising in her throat. She was standing and gazing mindlessly into her mirror when Julie came into their room and put a slimy, wet hand against her bare neck.

Cybil recoiled. "Don't! Get away from me."

"Chee, what a grouch!" Julie responded.

"What is that stuff, anyway?" Cybil asked, afraid she might barf all over Julie's enthusiasm.

"It's my new facial," she said as she began to smear the slime over her face. "It's supposed to make me gorgeous."

"Don't count on it." Cybil wiped the disgusting goo from her neck and shoulder.

"I hope you're not going to spend the rest of this year a grouch because of—hey, I thought I was your friend. But you don't need me. So, fine. I can handle that. Just don't ruin everyone's good time while you fight it out alone!"

Cybil watched her friend as she finished covering her face and then wiped the excess slime from her fingertips. She busied herself making her bed and selecting clothing for the day, ignoring Cybil's gaze. Cybil had been indifferent to Julie's feelings before, and Julie had always been either oblivious to it or quick to forgive. This new reaction confused her.

"I'm sorry," Cybil began.

"No reason to be. I don't need your problems." Julie's pout was transformed into a condescending sneer. She lifted her chin and made an indignant exit.

Cybil stood stunned. She ducked into the bathroom, found an empty shower stall and turned the water on. Her skin still felt parched from the night before. She fought an urge to repeat the scene, then sat on the dressing bench. Steam from the shower condensed on her face and mixed with her tears.

Before long the bathroom filled with girls waiting for the next available shower. One of them knocked on the latched metal door and shouted, "Hey, who's in there? Give some of the rest of us a chance."

Cybil dried her tears, reached into the shower and turned it off, and exited the stall, in wet pajamas but obviously unbathed.

"What gives, Renwick?" the girl waiting outside asked. "Are you all right?"

"I'm super," she answered, rushing past.

Back in her room, Cybil worked hard ignoring Julie. She threw her blankets up over her bed and straightened them haphazardly, sniffling back tears. She picked up from the day before and began sorting and stuffing dirty clothes into a large laundry basket in her closet. She reached for a pants hanger, pulling at it angrily; then, weeping with frustration, she ripped the hanger off the rod and threw it across the room.

"Hey, watch it, girl," Julie said as she dodged.

"*You* watch it — *girl*." Cybil glared. In a moment the anger that had consumed her melted, and the agony of her hurt took its place. She sank back onto the desk behind her.

"I'm sorry." She began to sob. She put both her hands to her face and cried into them. "I'm so sorry, Julie. Let's talk. I need to talk about this to somebody." She felt Julie's arms embrace her, and she let her head fall to rest against her friend's shoulder. "Please . . . "

_____Nineteen

Jeff had not wanted to leave Maggie so quickly after having been given such good news. Flying away from her at that moment had been like leaving paradise for purgatory. Coming back was all the sweeter, though, and he anticipated their reunion with schoolboy eagerness. Bad weather in Norfolk delayed his return flight for six hours. Not long enough to go home and relax, but way too long to hang around an airport alone. Hang around he did, however.

He called Maggie to explain and told her not to try to meet him. The flight, which should have arrived there early evening, was now expected to land after midnight. He didn't want her out at that hour in freezing temperatures.

"But I want to come."

"It'll be after midnight . . . "

"I know. But I'm bored to death. It's something to do."

"Honey. Don't push it, please. It won't get me there any quicker. There's no point in *both* of us freezing to death. Okay?"

"All right, but wake me when you get here."

"That's a promise."

The six-hour flight seemed twice that long. The engines droned on and on. He tried to read, but Maggie's image—smiling, joyous—drowned out the words. He envied those who could sleep sitting up. The woman next to him had pressed a pillow against the window and rested her head on it, and hadn't moved since. In the end, he asked the flight attendant for earphones and watched the last half of *Karate Kid II*.

The roads from the airport were slick with ice, and a sleety rain froze on the taxi's windshield.

"Not fit for a polar bear out there." Jeff tried to make small talk with the cabbie.

"It's about as bad as it gets here. Where are you from?"

"New York originally."

"Then you've seen worse."

"Oh, yeah. I've lived in L.A. for several years. I'd forgotten."

The hotel doorman pulled his coat collar up around his neck before stepping out into the cold. He stomped his feet as he opened Jeff's door. His breath turned white and obscured what little of his face was visible between his hat and wool scarf.

"Any bags, sir?" he asked.

"No. Thank you." Both men ran to the hotel door, the doorman taking the handle, then stepping back for Jeff to enter. *What a job*, Jeff thought as he pressed a five-dollar bill into the man's hand.

A sleepy desk clerk nodded as Jeff crossed the lobby to the elevators. A vacuum hummed, and a young woman in Levi's and a college sweatshirt moved out of the way as Jeff stepped over the electric cord.

The hotel room was dark except for a reading lamp that was part of the bed's headboard. Apparently Maggie had been reading when she fell asleep. Every pillow in the room was piled in one spot at the head of the bed, and Maggie was turned sideways, her body sprawled across them. Her book lay open, face down, a few inches from her fingertips. She stirred but didn't waken as he entered the room.

Jeff quickly undressed and slid under the warm blankets next to her. He brushed her hair away from her face and kissed her sweetly. She uttered something that sounded like "Hi, Dad," then turned and pulled the blankets up over her shoulder and settled down under them. Her eyes were still closed and her breathing slow and even.

"Maggie," he whispered. When she didn't respond, he reached up and turned out the light.

"Hi, Dad," he repeated to himself. Was that what she'd said? He liked it. He looked at Maggie's face and wondered if he should try again to waken her. He decided not. He gently wrapped an arm around her waist and fell fast asleep.

He woke a few minutes later with Maggie kissing him. She had pulled his undershirt up and ran her long, smooth fingernails through the thick hair on his chest.

"Hello," he said, at once fully awake.

"Why didn't you wake me when you got here?" she asked.

"Are you kidding? I tried. You said 'Hi, Dad' and turned over and went back to sleep."

"I did not."

"You most certainly did."

" 'Hi, Dad,' huh? Did you like that?"

"It sounded pretty good."

"Pretty good, my foot! You liked it." She pulled her arms from around his chest and began poking at his middle.

"Don't, honey, that tickles. All right, all right, I liked it."

She stopped her teasing and wrapped her arms around him again.

He felt the silky softness of her pajamas against his skin. They kissed and snuggled down under the covers.

Jeff turned the corner from the hall and entered the treatment room. Maggie was already on the table. A nurse directed him to a stool next to her, and he pulled it closer to the table. He leaned over her first, kissed her, and whispered "I love you" for only her to hear, then took her hand and sat down. The room was bigger than it needed to be and was lined with strange equipment—cold white and stainless steel boxes set on black wheels and covered with dials and gauges and electric cords. Two women dressed in white busied themselves around the table where Maggie lay.

The doctor came in, wearing a sterile green gown, and greeted them both.

"This is the easiest part of the procedure for you, Mrs. Perry. You'll only feel some gentle nudging. It'll be a matter of a few minutes and we'll be done. Then the nurses will turn you on your stomach. You'll remain that way for four hours. Then you can go back to your hotel and rest."

He sat on a stool at the end of the table and pulled a rolling cart next to him. He unwrapped a petri dish from sterile cloths and opened it, extracting the container's contents into an oversized syringe.

Jeff squeezed Maggie's hand and looked away.

"It doesn't hurt," she whispered.

"I know."

"There, we're done," the doctor said, withdrawing the instrument.

"That was easy," she said, smiling sweetly once the nurses left them alone.

"Easy for you," Jeff replied.

"Poor baby! I'm sorry you must suffer so."

They both laughed.

All that was left was waiting. It would be two weeks before tests would confirm that their embryo — their infant — had indeed properly implanted itself in the lining of Maggie's uterus — or had not.

"It's going to be a long two weeks," he said, relaxing.

"Yes," Maggie whispered. "Would it be better for you to go home where you have work to do? It'd go faster."

"And leave you here?" He felt a frown creep across his brow. "No, I don't think so."

Maggie reached for his hand, and Jeff inched his chair closer to her so they could touch without effort. "I brought church work to do — you know those Christmas figures I'm enbroidering for the children's nativity scene. I know you wouldn't want to go, but I'll be fine, and if the guys need you . . ."

"I'm due for a vacation."

"Since when do budding rock stars get vacations?"

He stood suddenly and walked to the window.

"What's wrong? You weren't conning me when you said you made your flight, were you? How'd the session go?"

"It went well. But that part of my life seems trivial now."

"It shouldn't. It isn't trivial. You're good. You also earn a good living. No one can ask more than that."

"Good living, sure. As long as I'm willing to teach, and write music for others to record, and a jillion other 'no name — no fame' jobs."

"I know you better than that. You like to teach and write, and you're not in it for the fame or the money. Well, maybe the money." She was grinning and winked at him when their eyes met. They both laughed.

"What I want is to succeed, and success in this business is spelled fame and big bucks."

"And you'll make it. I know it."

He walked back to her bed, rubbed her back gently with one hand, then leaned down and kissed her. "I wish I had your faith in me." Jeff paused momentarily. "Maggie," he said carefully. "You're counting too much on this working."

"No, I'm not, 'cause it's going to work."

"You don't know that." Jeff felt a familiar ache inside him. Maggie was going to be hurt again. There were so many other procedures, treatments that were also going to work and didn't. Thank goodness Maggie was strong and resilient. She could handle another disappointment; but handle it or not, she would hurt, and that did worry him. She'd seen enough pain. They'd both seen enough pain over this.

The Gallaghers were leaving the lab when Jeff and Maggie arrived for her daily blood test. "Are you finished already?" Maggie asked.

Cliff seemed agitated, and Patrice looked as if she was in a fog.

"The doctor wanted to see me today," she replied. "He asked us to come in early. He did the blood test himself this morning."

Maggie swallowed hard and tightened her grip around Jeff's hand. "And?" she asked.

"Maggie, we're pregnant!"

Maggie pulled away from Jeff and offered her hand to Patrice. She could hardly speak. "Oh, Patrice." She wrapped her arms around her newest friend's shoulders. "I'm happy for you."

"Congratulations," Jeff said, pumping Cliff's hand.

"I wish I could tell you how it feels," Patrice added as she looked first at Maggie, then Jeff. "But in a couple of days you'll be getting the same news." She hugged Maggie with vigor and took her husband's arm. "We did it! It's so incredible — we really did it! We're going to celebrate with a whopper, jumbo fries, milkshake. Hang the calories, I'm starved," she said. "Good luck, you two," she called back as they rounded a corner and stepped out of sight.

Maggie's eyes were still wet when Jeff turned his attention back to her.

"Tears of joy?" he asked.

"Honestly I *am* happy for them. How could I be anything else?" She wiped her face with a tissue she'd pulled from her purse. "But I wish it were me. Selfish, huh?" And the tears spilled out onto her cheeks.

Jeff took her shoulders with one arm and pulled her close to him. He kissed her forehead and held her several seconds longer. *One more test*, he thought. *One more of how many*? It had seemed like thousands already.

"Let's go and get this done," he said, directing her toward the lab door.

Jeff pulled the hotel room door closed behind him. He turned on the light and walked to the window to close the curtains. They'd been downstairs for dinner; it had grown dark while they were gone. He looked at his watch and was surprised at how late it was. They'd stayed in the hotel's dining room and talked while the happy-hour crowd came and went. Several young airmen from Langley Field were there with their dates. They were boisterous and cheerful. Maggie and Jeff laughed when one flyer took the waiter's tray and served the drinks to his table himself. With great flourish he dipped the tray low in front of each of the ladies and asked their pleasure.

It felt good to laugh and talk. They talked about everything except babies and doctors and daily labwork routines. It was almost eleven when they returned to their room.

"You'd better get to bed, Maggie," he said. "It's getting late."

The phone rang and Jeff picked it up.

"Mr. Perry?" the voice asked.

"Yes."

"Doctor would like to see your wife and you tomorrow, early."

Jeff listened carefully and wrote "Lab, 7:00 A.M. Doctor" on a scratch pad near the phone and held it up for Maggie to see.

He watched her as the smile on her lips spelled out happy news.

"Mr. Perry?" the voice questioned again.

"Yes, yes. I'm here. Yes, we'll be there. Thank you." And he hung up.

He took a deep breath as he watched his wife get high on excitement. He felt the nerve endings along his backbone tingle, and he fought to keep his own excitement to himself.

"Maggie, this isn't necessarily going to go the same way the Gallaghers' news did."

"Don't say that." She stood and reached around his neck and gently rested her head on his chest. "It will. I know it will. The tests were positive today, and he wants to repeat them himself. Otherwise we'd have our usual appointment with the technician at eight."

Jeff pulled her close to him and kissed the top of her head. They undressed quickly, said their prayers together, and then Jeff urged Maggie into bed. He hung her clothes on hangers along with his own and put them in the closet. In a few minutes he climbed into bed beside her. She went to sleep quickly; he didn't. After an hour or so he got up, stood for a while at the window, watching the lights flash below, coloring the window glass red and gold. Somewhere a siren screamed. He pulled the curtains shut and turned on a reading lamp and sat down to read. He dozed off and was wakened later by a sound that sickened him—Maggie's frightened moans.

Jeff rubbed the sleep from his eyes, came to his feet, moving quickly, and reached the light switch near the door and turned it on. Maggie was on her side facing him, her legs pulled up against her body. Her eyes were wide and full of fear.

"Maggie, what's wrong?"

"Jeff, I think I'm bleeding."

Jeff pulled away the blankets that covered her. Blood streaked the inside legs of her pajamas. Powerful bands of fear gripped his chest, and he gasped for air. Maggie's moans brought him back to the task at hand. He covered her again and lifted the telephone to his ear. He continued to meter air to his lungs as if it were being rationed. When the operator answered he whispered hoarsely, "This is Jeff Perry in room 214. We need an ambulance." He went to the bathroom, dampened a towel, and returned to wipe perspiration from Maggie's brow and her neck. Then, without leaving her side, he reached behind him and took the tiny vial of consecrated oil from his shaving kit bag and turned back toward her.

He knelt by the bed, laid his arm across the mattress just above her head, and looked closely at her contorted face.

"I'm sorry," he whispered.

"You were right. This isn't going to work for us!" she cried.

"No, no. Don't say it now; we'll see what the doctor says," he said in a slow, even monotone. "It's going to be all right; I'm here and it's going to be all right. I'm going to give you a blessing, if that's all right," he said as his fingers tightened around the bottle's tiny black lid.

"Yes, please," she responded and closed her eyes.

He watched closely as he tipped the bottle and a single drop of oil flowed onto Maggie's forehead. He rubbed it into her skin. Then he humbly knelt beside her and laid his hands on her head.

Later at the center, their worst fears were confirmed.

"I'm sorry, Mr. Perry," the doctor began as he directed Jeff into a small office in the emergency room area of the medical center.

Jeff sat down, leaned forward, and rested his head in his hands. His eyes were raw and sore. "What happened?" he finally asked.

"I don't know for sure. Has your wife miscarried before?"

"No. She's never been pregnant . . . before. How is she now?"

"I've sedated her. She'll rest soundly. She didn't lose a lot of blood. It always looks like more than it is. She'll feel a little weakness for a few days. You can take her home tomorrow."

The doctor relaxed back in his chair. Jeff was aware that the older man was watching him intently. After a moment the doctor spoke again. "You and your wife remain excellent candidates for *in vitro*, Mr. Perry."

"What?" Jeff said looking directly at the doctor for the first time.

"This miscarriage was unfortunate, but I'm convinced after examining her just now, and after watching her progress over the past three weeks, that it was just a fluke. If she could get pregnant she would not be prone to miscarry. The fact that *in vitro* fertilization worked for you once makes you excellent candidates for it to work again."

"No!" Jeff rose from his chair.

"I only suggest it because you both seem to want . . . "

"No. We won't do this again. I don't want you to mention this to Maggie. We tried. It didn't work. That's the end of it."

The doctor was surprised at his reaction. "I . . . uh, I'm afraid it's too late."

"Too late?" Jeff asked.

"I've already told your wife. She asked and I told her I thought you had a very good chance of succeeding next time."

Jeff stared at the doctor for a long moment without saying a word. Then he sat back into his chair and stared at nothing. Tears filled his eyes. He pulled a handkerchief from his pocket and wiped them away.

"If she wants to try again, surely you can't deny her . . . "

"I can," Jeff whispered. "I can because I love her." He leaned toward the doctor and spoke clearly in spite of his quivering voice. "You feel compassion for our desire for a child and say to yourself you can help us. And that's great—for you. It's great for those who are helped as well. But you can't ache for us the way I ache for Maggie as each bright new avenue turns into a dead end. I'm sorry, Doctor, but I can deny her torturing herself again. I can and I will."

Maggie pulled a suitcase off the shelf in the closet. She opened it on the bed and began arranging folded clothing in it.

Jeff opened and closed drawers and cupboards in the bathroom. "The bathroom's clear," he said as he switched the light off and pulled the door closed behind him. He began opening and closing drawers in the desk.

"There's nothing in the desk," Maggie said.

"It won't take a minute to check it, anyway."

Maggie stopped packing and turned toward him. "I didn't put anything in the desk."

Jeff pulled a new application to the clinic from the bottom drawer. "What's this?"

Maggie slumped onto the bed. "I started to fill it out," she said, "but I decided to take it home and talk to you about it later."

Jeff gave the piece of paper a sideways toss into the wastebasket. "I think we'd better talk about it now," he said.

"All right."

"I'm not going to change my mind," Jeff insisted.

Maggie's shoulders drooped, and she looked forlorn. He looked away. He fought an urge to take her in his arms and tell her it would be okay; that it would never be okay so long as "okay" meant they'd someday have a baby of their own; that she had to give up that dream before it destroyed her, before it destroyed them both.

He measured his words carefully. "Maggie, it's time we faced this. We're not going to have a—"

"No!" she screamed. "Don't say it."

"We're not going to have a baby," he said all the louder.

"Don't say it," she repeated as if she hadn't heard him. "The doctor says we have a good chance if we try again."

"No, Maggie. We're not going to try again." He metered his words and spoke softly.

"Why?" she screamed, lashing out at him. Tears ran down her cheeks and mascara lay in pools under her eyes. The combination of anger and black stains gave her face a fierceness Jeff had never seen before. He stepped forward and reached for her.

She responded with clenched fists that came down hard on his chest and shoulders. "Why, why?" she repeated. Then she backed away. "You don't want a baby. That's it, isn't it? This has all worked out great for you! You and your career. Babies don't fit your image—Mister Show Biz, Mister Big Rock Star . . . "

Jeff felt pain stab at him. It was pain he had endured for over a year—all the time they'd spent trying. The memories caused pain in themselves—effort had become desperation—and now this. "Don't, Maggie," he said. "Let's not say things we'll regret."

Maggie grabbed up a piece of clothing from the bed and frantically wiped her face. She backed away from him. "You couldn't want it as badly as I do or you wouldn't be willing to give up now," she whispered.

"That's not fair."

Maggie wheeled around and faced him again. "Isn't it? Why, then? Why are you willing to give up?"

Jeff stepped forward until his face was inches from hers. "Because there's a limit," he answered. "There's a bottom line to every situation, and we've reached it. Look at us, Maggie. Look what's happened to us. We never fight like this. In three years of marriage you've never said a hurtful thing to me—and now you're accusing me of putting my career before my family!"

Jeff watched Maggie's face contort with pain. He put arms out to bring her to him, but she slapped him and backed away.

"Don't touch me. You have what you wanted, you and your recordings and your long-haired cronies. Just don't include me in your plans ever again."

"Maggie!" He reached for her but she drew back as if he were repulsive to her. Her look cut through him and left him weak and helpless.

"I'm leaving." She let her head drop like a bull ready to charge and elbowed her way past him. She threw what was left of her clothes into her suitcase and slammed the lid closed. She pulled her coat off its hanger and her purse from the dresser and was out of the door before Jeff could move.

"For heaven's sake, Maggie, will you stop this foolishness." He followed her down the long hallway. He caught up with her when she slowed to allow a woman with a small child to pass her. He tried to take her bag, but she jerked it from him, then stopped to face him. She watched the woman unlock her door and direct the child inside. She waited until the door latched closed.

"That's what's wrong with you—with us, Jeff. My feelings are not *foolishness*. I'm *not* a child. You've babied and smothered me until I feel like a child sometimes. I even act like one, but I'm not. I have feelings about this—our life—our problems. I have choices—I can make decisions. I have a mind. I can think. I'm even smart . . . oh, what a stupid thing to say!" She turned and walked away from him, taking long, purposeful strides.

Jeff watched her until she reached the elevator and pushed the button. When the doors opened immediately, he turned and ran toward her, reaching the elevator too late to stop it. He cursed as he pushed the button with no response.

He opened the door to the stairwell and, clutching the rail, flew down the stairs two and three at a time. He felt panic building in him. He stumbled once, losing precious seconds. His bruised shin throbbed as he leapt down the steps all the faster. He pushed the lobby door open in time to see the doorman help Maggie into a cab.

"Where'd she tell the cabbie to take her?" he asked once he was outside.

"I couldn't say."

"Hey, man, that's my wife. You've seen us together . . . "

"Yes, Mister Perry, but I didn't hear her say."

———— *Twenty*

Jeff looked up to see the cab driver shaking his head as he watched him in the rearview mirror. A grown man crying is something even a cabbie doesn't see very often, Jeff reasoned.

"Woman trouble?"

Jeff laughed pathetically while blowing his nose. "You got it."

"Wife? Girlfriend?"

"Wife."

"Take my advice, buddy. Whatever she says you did, admit it and apologize. Women go for the humble type. Fighting it out ain't worth it."

"I just wanted to protect her. I didn't want her to be hurt any more. What's so terrible?" Jeff muttered, not really for the driver to hear.

"She left you for that? I figured another guy or somethin'. Or another girl — a lot of that goin' around. Women — go figure 'em."

It was Friday and servicemen packed the air terminal, on standby for a cheap flight home. Jeff sighed as he stood at the end of a long line waiting to check in. *She's probably here, but how will I ever find her in this mess?* he questioned. His eyes searched first the lines nearby, then waiting rooms on both sides of him. The video display announced gate 11 for his flight. She'd be there waiting — he hoped. He handed the clerk both tickets and got two boarding passes.

The gate 11 waiting area filled up fast. His eyes quickly inventoried each face. He saw Maggie nowhere among them. Jeff felt his chest tighten, and he sank back against a pillar.

Artificial heat and moisture weighted the air. A cleaning lady ran a vacuum over carpeting in the empty waiting area a few yards down. That and the noise of people talking and the almost constant intrusion of the PA system made Jeff's head pound. When the cleaning woman finished and pushed her cart past him, Jeff stopped her, gave her a dollar, and asked her to check the ladies' restroom for Maggie.

"No one answers to that name," she said when she returned. She stuffed the dollar in her pocket and walked away.

He turned back toward the waiting area and blindly searched for a seat. He felt dazed and a little sick as he walked toward the far side of the room, where a few seats remained empty. As he rounded a large pillar he saw Maggie sitting with her back to him, staring out of the observation windows toward the airfield.

He felt happy and sad and frightened all at the same time. A part of him wanted to run to her; another part wanted to run away. He looked at the crowd sitting around them. How could they talk here? What could he say to her with others pressing against them listening? He rushed toward her, but stopped ten feet behind her to watch for a moment and think. Her tightly curled hair had escaped its clip on the side nearest him and bushed out in that direction. He could see traces of mascara smeared across her temple. She had removed the colorful scarf she'd spent so much time tying that morning, and had it clutched in her fist. Her shoulders drooped and her breathing was jerky and uneven.

Suddenly she turned and saw him. "Jeff," she said reaching toward him. He hurried to her and took her hand. She was sitting at the end of a long row of chairs. The one next to her was taken by an older lady who watched them closely. Jeff looked at her, then at the others around them. He looked toward the few seats that'd been empty moments ago, but they were all full now. There wasn't even standing room large enough for any privacy. He frowned and sank down in front of Maggie, sitting on his heels, her hand still in his.

"Thank goodness you're here," he said in a whisper.

"Oh Jeff, where else would I be? I'm so ashamed. I shouldn't have left like that. I just . . . "

"No, don't. I'm sorry too."

"We need to talk about this." Maggie looked pained and shook her head. "When I think of the things I said to you, I . . . "

"It's okay, sweetheart, I know."

The grandmotherly lady sitting next to them looked first at one and then the other, as if she were watching a tennis match. Jeff looked at her and she grinned and looked away momentarily.

"We can't talk here." He surveyed the room again, then looked back at his wife. "There's no place . . . " His whisper faded to nothing and he squeezed her hand. "I want to hold you close so badly right now I ache inside." He could see the old woman nodding and smiling, trying to appear as if she were looking away. Maggie just smiled, apparently unaware of her neighbor's interest.

Uniformed attendants busied themselves at the desk a few feet away, and one now removed the velvet-covered chain that separated them from the crowd.

"We'll be boarding soon. There'll be time for talk once we're aboard and settled." Jeff turned back toward Maggie. She'd apparently been staring at him, a fact that obviously pleased their observant friend. He smiled warmly and she leaned forward suddenly and kissed him unashamedly. When she finished, she backed away only centimeters and said, "Thanks for being so understanding." Even without taking his eyes off Maggie, Jeff could see the old woman edge closer and stare intently at them. *What the heck*, he thought. *What're airports for anyway?* He reached behind Maggie's soft curly head and pulled her to him, kissing her generously. He thought he sensed the woman applauding beside them. That was okay. He felt like applauding too.

Home offered no comfort for Jeff. Maggie hadn't left him, and life was beautiful. But even a beautiful life could be imperfect. They still had some important decisions to make, and all their talk since arriving home yesterday hadn't seemed to resolve anything. The Southern California beach air was cool, in some ways cooler than that in Norfolk. He pulled on a sweatshirt and wandered out to a three-foot retaining wall forty feet from their condo. He eased himself onto the wall's upper edge and let his feet dangle down over it.

He jumped down from the wall and began running along the water's edge. Water and sand spurted out ahead of him as his feet hit the ground in precise rhythm. He watched the sprays of sand fan out in front of each footfall and wondered if every grain really were numbered. He felt absent, uncounted. His heart rate increased until it was hard for him to breathe, but he pressed on. Once he was past the point of exhaustion, his head cleared and his thoughts came back to Maggie.

She loved him. He knew that. He'd always known it, almost from the first moment they met. He smiled as he thought of her swooning over him. It had amused him at first—until he started to fall in love with her. Then it became sweet and precious to him. Since then their feelings for each other had matured and strengthened until he knew they would never end.

Had he loved her too much? Was it possible to love someone too much? She'd said he babied her. She'd meant dominated. He did dominate their relationship. He thought she liked it. He laughed at his own ignorance. He remembered his father's efforts to rule at home. His father was a good man, and his mother complied, sometimes. But she didn't like it. *You've come a long way, baby*. Jeff laughed again. If Maggie wanted more freedom in their relationship, why hadn't she said so? The picture of her adoring face invaded his thoughts, and his eyes flooded with tears. *Because she'd do anything to please you. Because she loves you too much.*

Twenty-One

"Aren't you going to tell Mike?" Julie asked as Cybil hurriedly pulled the Velcro closed on her snow boots and threw a fringed woolen scarf around her neck.

"No." She snapped her jacket and grabbed her cap.

"Why not?"

" 'Cause he wouldn't want to know."

"This is the eighties, girl. You don't have to sneak around back alleys and keep this to yourself. He's responsible — let him help pay."

"I may tell him later, once I decide what to do."

"Decide? Are you crazy? There's only one thing to do."

"Get rid of it."

"Yes."

"That sounds so easy, but it's wrong, isn't it? Anyway, I don't think I could live with it," Cybil answered. "We had kittens once. I remember their mother . . . " She stopped talking and looked back at Julie. She had really tried hard to keep those kittens alive. Unfortunately *this* situation had a flip side. She would suffer more than Sassy had, and so would her family. Her reaction to that thought surprised her. She felt weak, and her freckled body was covered with goose bumps.

"What?" Julie asked. "You remember what?"

"Nothing. I was just thinking out loud."

"Girl, you *are* crazy. There's no reason you should have this baby."

Cybil pulled the cap down over her ears.

"Listen to me," Julie began again. "Make it easy on yourself, okay?"

"I'll think about it," Cybil promised. "I've got to go. I'm going to be late for class."

"Cybil," Julie called after her as she left the room. She followed Cybil out the door. There were other girls in the hall waiting for the elevator. Julie looked at Cybil and simply said, "Do it."

"We'll see," Cybil answered.

Seated in Reverend Callahan's office at the Women's Health Center because Julie pushed until she agreed, Cybil still didn't feel good about it. But she was relieved to have someone make that choice for her. Julie had even called and made the appointment for the required counseling. She had also made an appointment to have the abortion the same day, and had come with her to drive her back to the dorm after it was over.

The desk and office were obviously used by a variety of people. There were copies of several degrees on the wall behind, each one bearing a different name. The plastic nameplate on the desk was one from which the name could be removed by sliding it out of the end. Cybil could imagine a pile of the removable names in a drawer somewhere in the desk.

Mr. Callahan had two personal items he displayed prominently. One was a wooden plaque that bore an inscribed verse from the Bible: "Inasmuch as ye have done it unto one of the least of these . . . , ye have done it unto me." Cybil tried not to think about what that meant. The other was a family portrait. Cybil turned it toward her and looked at it intently. It was of a minister and his wife and five children. She had seen the minister in the waiting room just after the receptionist had directed her back to his office. A man and woman had come into the waiting room and had asked to talk to him. The man awkwardly held a small baby and the woman stood next to him, a diaper bag slung casually over her shoulder. They drew her attention because they didn't belong there.

"Harry, Virginia." Reverend Callahan greeted them, taking the man's free hand. "Boy, he's getting big, isn't he?" he said, looking at the baby.

Both parents beamed.

"What are you doing here?" the reverend asked.

"We tried to call you at home, but . . . "

Cybil missed the rest of the conversation, as the reception room door closed behind them. But she saw and heard enough to know that the couple was happy with their baby. *Babies do make people happy*, she told herself, and that thought pulled at her.

The office door opened and interrupted her reverie. She jumped.

"I'm sorry," Reverend Callahan said. "Did I startle you?"

"That's okay. I guess I'm kind of nervous."

"Don't be." He touched her shoulder on the way to his chair.

He introduced himself, and she noted he was soft-spoken, sweet, and shy. But he had no trouble in communicating with her. In fact, he was good at it. She had assumed that this visit would be cold—indifferent, sort of. But she was wrong. She felt he cared what happened to her, and soon she told him everything she had endured since she first knew she was pregnant.

"You're young, single, and pregnant, and you can't deal with that," Reverend Callahan summed it up.

Why does that sound so spineless? she thought. "Look, Reverend, if I have an abortion my parents won't ever know. That alone is reason enough to want it."

"That alone? Does that mean you have other reasons?"

"Well, yes. The timing's all wrong—in more than one way." She turned nervously in her chair. "I mean, . . . well . . . I'm too young for a baby. I can't take care of it. I'm in school . . . it would ruin everything." She looked for agreement. She found sympathy, but that was all. Adding to her argument, she continued, "The world doesn't need another unwanted baby."

"There are others who would gladly take your child and give him a good home."

"That's probably true, but it's not easy to think about."

"I know. I'm just saying that when you use the word 'unwanted,' you must ask yourself, 'By whom?' Someone will want him, I'll guarantee that."

She stood and walked to the window. Outside, a group of school children had gathered to exchange Christmas cards. She sat again quickly, not wanting to be seen. The Reverend Callahan continued. "You said the timing was wrong in other ways. How?"

"Because of school. I'd have to stay out next quarter."

The reverend frowned, and Cybil wondered what he was thinking.

"When will you graduate—if you have no interruptions?"

"Three years."

"June?"

"Yes."

"If you have the baby, then you'd graduate a quarter later." He paused momentarily. "You said you were afraid of what would happen if your parents knew about your pregnancy."

"No. Not afraid."

"Your parents, are they harsh with you?" She didn't answer. "Some parents are, of course. They can be very tough on a daughter who's broken their rules. I can understand fear in that case."

"I said I wasn't afraid of them!" She felt suddenly angry and wished she hadn't let Julie drag her over here. She wanted to be somewhere else, anywhere else.

"What, then?"

She turned away from him and began to cry. "I don't know." She did know. "They'll . . . be hurt. They'll be disappointed." She stared out of the window. "I'll feel like a slut." She turned back toward him and added emphatically, "They won't make me feel guilty, but I will."

"Do you feel guilty now?"

"Yes."

"Because of your parents."

"No . . . yes! . . . in a way."

Mr. Callahan paused momentarily, then spoke again. "How would your parents feel if they knew you had an abortion?"

"Terrible."

"Worse than if they knew you were pregnant?"

"Much worse."

"They'd be disappointed . . . hurt?"

"Yes."

"Would you feel guilty then?"

"I suppose so . . . yes."

"More than you do now?"

"Yes, much more."

"Even though they wouldn't know."

"If they didn't know, it wouldn't matter."

"They don't know you're pregnant, and it matters."

Cybil felt tears swim in her eyes again. They spilled out onto her cheeks, and her nose began to run. The young minister stood and came around his desk, offered her a tissue, and took her by the shoulders, directing her to the chairs at the back of the room. They sat there together, her limp shoulders cradled in his arms, until she stopped crying. When she moved he released her, and she stood.

"I . . . I'm sorry." She wanted to say that she could handle this, and take on a courageous pose. But she couldn't. She couldn't handle it alone. "What am I going to do?"

The minister returned to his chair behind his desk. "You have several options, Cybil." He glanced at her paperwork before him. "I see you've already made an appointment for an abortion. If you feel you want it, that's one option. But," he quickly added, "you can have the baby and keep it. What about his father? Does he know?"

"No."

"Is he a student?"

"Yes, with another year of undergraduate work, and vet school. This would ruin him."

"He needs to make that choice."

"I don't think so."

Rich thought of his fears a lifetime ago when he and Penny were expecting Bobby—a precious child. He pressed a forefinger between his brows and rubbed gently as he thought. "Other students have finished with families. It's rough, but they make it."

"I don't want to get married."

"I see. You can still keep the baby. That's not as unheard of as it once was, and with your parents' help it's not impossible."

"No. I don't want this baby," she whispered. "I know that's selfish . . . "

"It isn't selfish, Cybil. It's very human and honest. We often tell ourselves we're not ready for one challenge or another, that the time is not right. It would've been better, of course, if you'd realized that before you became pregnant. But one never goes back."

He watched her so closely that she felt uncomfortable and turned sideways in her chair. Then he went on. "Well, all right. You don't want this baby. There are still several options left. There are a number of good homes around the state, private and public, where a young unmarried girl can live with other girls, like herself, until the baby is born. The baby is then put up for adop—"

The room seemed to become too warm to bear, and Cybil wanted to leave—now. "I'm sorry; I can't think right now. I've got to go." She rose and shoved her hands deeply into her jacket pockets. "I won't do it—I mean, I won't do it now." Why she felt compelled to say that, she didn't know, except it was important that he know it. She felt shaken, more shaken than she had before she talked to him. Her hands trembled and she grasped the pocket linings in each fist and squeezed tightly as if they were all she had to cling to.

"Good. We can talk later if you wish. I'll send a list of agencies home with you. You can look at them at your leisure. Miss Renwick, you're little more than a child yourself, and you're not alone in this world."

He stood, came around the desk, and leaned against its front edge.

"Your parents are kind people?"

"Yes."

"They're loving people, too, I'll bet."

"Yes."

"Tell them!" He paused and looked directly into her eyes. "Tell them before you have to suffer another moment alone. Let them help you with this decision."

"It's going to be hard." She blinked back tears and wiped the back of her hand across her nose.

"I know." He offered her another tissue. "Would you like me to talk to them?"

That would be easier, she thought. *But easier for whom?* Certainly not for her parents. Her thoughts surprised her. How often in her lifetime had she been concerned about what was best for someone else?

"No. No, thank you. I can handle it." She shook the reverend's hand, then walked toward the door. In two giant steps, he was there to open it for her. He handed her the list of agencies and his business card.

"If you need anything—anything! I mean it!—call me." He stopped her momentarily. "Please, put my number in your wallet now—where it won't be lost." He waited while she slid the card under the plastic that covered Mike's picture. "Call me. Anytime. Please!"

Julie's eyes widened in surprise when Cybil reappeared in the waiting room less than an hour after she left it.

"What gives?"

"I'm going home."

"What? . . . Are you crazy?"

"Let's not make a scene here, Julie. I'll explain in the car."

Julie hesitated, then complied. In the car, she continued, "Now, what happened?"

"I can't do it yet. I need time to think."

"You've had time, and *more* thinking will only postpone the inevitable. It's that preacher you talked to. He's complicated this for you when it could be so simple." Julie turned away from her friend and emphatically folded her arms across her chest. Cybil could almost hear the "hrrumph" implied by her action.

"He was very kind and understanding." What Julie thought mattered to Cybil, and she ached at her friend's angry stare. This was hard enough. Why was she making it harder?

"I'll take you back to the dorm. I'm going to get enough clothes for the weekend, and I'm going home."

Julie turned back to her friend. "And what happens then, Cybil? Huh? You run home to Mommy and Daddy who always fix everything, only they can't fix this, and then what?"

"I don't know. Maybe they can't fix it, but they'll help. They'll make it easier, somehow."

"You're living in a dream world, girl."

Their conversation had become hostile and had no real purpose. Cybil regretted that. "Listen, Julie. I've really appreciated your support through all of this. I'm going to need lots more. You've got to accept my decision, whatever it is, and still be my friend." Cybil had stopped the car and turned off the ignition. Large flakes of snow stuck to the windshield. Cybil watched them gather in wet white clumps. The street lamps came on, illuminating the dorm parking lot with pale circles of light. Julie waited only a moment, and then nodded grimly. "Friends," she said.

Twenty-Two

"You know, it's weird," Cybil said after greeting her parents, "but it seems like a long time since I was home last."

"It's only been a couple of weeks since Thanksgiving. Everything's all right at school, isn't it, dear?" Mrs. Renwick asked.

"Fine," Cybil lied. The Christmas tree stood in front of the bay window and was decorated with all the familiar ornaments her mother had been collecting over twenty years of marriage. Cinnamon and cloves simmered on the stove, filling the house with the scent of Christmas. _Mother's such a traditionalist_, Cybil thought. _Too bad life isn't really as safe and warm as this room feels._

"You only have another week before Christmas vacation. Why did you come all this way now? And you're not wearing Michael's pin."

Cybil unconsciously felt the front of her blouse where she would normally have pinned it. Except for the discussion she'd had with Julie over telling Mike about her pregnancy, she hadn't thought much about him lately. She'd deliberately left the pin at school. She didn't know why.

"Marianne, I'm sure Cybil could do without this third degree."

"No, Dad. It's all right. I don't mind." Cybil wanted desperately to blurt out her reason for coming home, but it was hard. She turned her head away from them as tears welled up in her eyes. "In fact, there's something I need to tell you."

"Now, Cybil, whatever it is, it can't be that bad. In fact, we don't even need to know it if you'd rather not tell us. We're not the snoopy kind. You're a big girl now and—"

"Wait a minute, Ralph. Don't stop her. If she needs to talk to us, we'll listen."

"Oh, Mamma!" Cybil fell into her mother's arms—an embrace that was long overdue.

"My goodness, child. You haven't cried like this since you were a little girl. What's the matter?"

136

"I'm afraid to tell you." They both sat down, still in each other's arms. Cybil looked at her mother through tear-filled eyes. "I don't want to hurt you."

"Sounds like girl talk to me." Her father eased his way out of the room.

"Sweetheart, don't worry about hurting me." The mother brushed hair out of her child's eyes. "Nothing could be that bad." She paused, then added, "Just say it, Cybil. That's the easiest way—just say it right out."

Cybil stopped crying, and wiped her face with a tissue. "I'm pregnant."

Her mother sat stunned and silent. Cybil watched her for a moment, then began to cry again.

"Oh, Mamma, I'm so sorry. I didn't want to have to tell you, but—"

"No, Cybil, . . . I'm sorry . . . I mean . . . I don't know what to say." She took Cybil in her arms and cried, too.

Cybil slept remarkably well in her own bed that night. She awoke the next morning to the sound of Sassy purring next to her. "Ooo, you sweet kitty," she cooed as she stroked the animal's soft fur. She pulled her pillow up against the headboard behind her and sat cross-legged on the bed. "Come here, you luscious ball of fluff. I've missed you so much." She cradled the cat in her arms and scratched her belly with tender fingers.

She was glad she'd come home. After her talk with her mother, she felt relieved. Her father hadn't stayed around long enough to hear what she'd said. Cybil could only assume that her mother had told him by now. She wondered what kind of confrontation she would have with him this morning—if any at all.

Breakfast was strange. The cat meowed for her food, and rubbed her back against Cybil's legs, and played underfoot as Cybil silently helped her mother set the table. There was a fresh layer of snow outside, and the windows were steamy. The aroma of coffee and sausage dominated her senses. She felt almost too warm and opened the window over the sink, which her mother promptly closed again, giving her a curious look. When her dad came into the kitchen, he gave his wife a squeeze around the waist and kissed her on the cheek. Then he stroked his daughter's hair and kissed the top of her head as he used to do when she was a little girl. Cybil fought back an urge to hug him. When he had walked away from her and sat down at the kitchen table, she felt sorry. Her father's hair was wet from his shower and slicked back, his skin was rosy from his after-shave. The familiar fragrance touched her and brought back memories of other Christmases when she'd spent her whole allowance on his favorite after-shave. She'd remember to buy him another bottle before she came back for Christmas next week.

Mr. Renwick adjusted his glasses and picked up the morning paper. "Did you see this, Marianne? There are two murders on the front page. Makes you wonder." He sipped the coffee that his wife put in front of him.

Cybil was numb. She had hoped she could talk to him this morning. He was going to ignore the whole thing if he could. How would that help her? Even her mother, who had been so willing to talk the night before, had grown silent.

They finished breakfast in idle chatter. When her father finished his second cup of coffee and stood to leave, Cybil gave him the hug she wished she'd given him earlier. He hugged her back and said, "Everything's going to be fine again, Punkin. You'll see."

Still clinging to him, she spoke through a profusion of tears. "I need you, Daddy. Please talk to me. Yell at me if you want, but don't ignore me. Please!"

"I have no desire to yell at you." He looked into her face. "Does that surprise you? Yelling is something a parent does when a child breaks Grandma's favorite vase—not at times like this."

Cybil was terrified that that might be all she would get from him. She'd have preferred yelling. "I don't know what to do next. I need you and Mom to help me."

Cybil's father had spoiled her; she knew that better than any of them. He'd spoiled her, not because he couldn't be bothered with her as some parents do—a sort of payoff for time not spent together—but because he could never face saying no. Confronting her bad behavior, which inevitably had come, had also been impossible for him. This new situation was another case of bad behavior he couldn't cope with. He looked evasive. "Sweetheart, . . . I, uh . . . I have to go to work now. I'll talk to you later. I can't be late this morning—a rush job for a special client . . . "

"But I've done some thinking about this," she began cautiously, watching as he buttoned his overcoat and checked his pockets for his car keys. "Would you like to hear what I want to do?"

"We don't need to hear it, Punkin. Whatever you decide is fine." He left the room, then came back, keys in hand. "Except," he added, "we think it would be unwise to keep the baby. That would be difficult for all of us. But whatever you want."

Cybil looked at her mother, who avoided her gaze. *She's caved in again—Mother always gives in to Daddy. How many times in my life have I counted on that? This time it's backfired.* She looked back at her father. *This is incredible,* she thought. *They're really going to ignore this.* Her tears were replaced by a pounding head and a rising anger.

She spoke slowly. "Would you like to know I'm considering an abortion?"

"Now we don't want to hear you talk like that," her father said, but he looked only slightly alarmed. "We don't want to hear of you doing something illegal or dangerous . . . "

"Where've you been? It's legal! And what would you like to hear?" The taste of coffee was still bitter in her mouth. "I know. You'd like to hear that it never happened."

"Of course . . . "

"Of course!" she shouted. "You're not going to help with this, are you? This is another one of precious little Cybil's silly tricks you'll choose to ignore. What happens, Dad, if I decide to keep the baby and come back here to raise it?"

"I don't know, Cybil. That would be hard . . . " His perplexed voice drifted off, his thought unfinished.

"Never mind! I've got the picture." She grabbed her coat and purse from the hook near the door.

"Cybil," she heard her mother call after her. She waved her off and threw herself into the driver's seat of her car.

The drive back to campus was colder than usual. She wore her warmest coat, but in her haste she had left her scarf and gloves. She'd left everything else she'd brought home for the weekend, too, and regretted it. She absently inventoried things she'd have to live without as if that were her biggest problem.

She was glad Julie wasn't home when she got back to their room. She had to think. She hadn't even removed her coat when she decided to take a walk to the commons for a cup of coffee and hopefully some solitude.

The chill felt good as Cybil stepped outside. She loosened the scarf around her neck and breathed in the fresh, cold air. It had snowed during the night, and the earlier snow that had turned to icy crust was covered by a new downy blanket. Workmen were out with large flat shovels clearing the campus streets and walkways, and Cybil smiled wanly at one of them as she skirted his work area, then stepped back onto the walk he'd already cleared.

A group of students in the quad had just begun to build a snowman. They had chosen a spot midway between the center walk and the curb. She sat on a nearby bench and watched it grow from the tiniest snowball to bigger than life. Cybil recognized the boy who seemed to be engineering the project as one of Mike's Alpha Gamm brothers. Cybil marveled at how willingly his compatriots followed his instructions. When they were finished, the structure seemed to have no form at all. It was a large white lump six feet tall at its highest point and eight feet long at the base.

The young artist stood back, examined his friends' work, and seemed pleased with what they had accomplished. Then he went to work. He cut and turned and shaped, removing pieces of icy snow as he went. He stopped frequently and stepped back to appraise his progress, then returned to his task with new inspiration. When he was satisfied he walked away, and with a wide sweeping gesture announced its completion. Friends and spectators, including Cybil, applauded wildly.

He had created a six-foot snowman complete with carrot nose and top hat. The happy fellow sported a Chamberlain State pennant in one bulky hand. The other hand gave a thumbs-up gesture, and a large booted foot was planted firmly across the face of State U's infamous bear.

The crowd that had gathered began to disperse. Even the artist, who seemed to relish the process, lost interest in the creation. He waved to Cybil as he passed by her bench and walked toward the coffee shop.

Cybil sat there for a long time staring at the ice sculpture. People passed by and laughed at the giant as the afternoon sun began to melt away his features. When the carrot nose fell Cybil hurried to replace it, at the same time resecuring the pennant in the monster's fading hand.

Cybil began to cry as she thought of the snowman disappearing completely, long before the coldness of the sunset could save it. Her tears were irrational and yet she had no control over them. She continued to stare at the huge ice statue, wiping furiously at her tears.

She reached for a tissue. The papers the reverend had given her were rolled into a tube and stuffed into her pocket. She pulled them out and unrolled them with shaking hands. Cybil's eyes focused on Reverend Callahan's signature at the bottom of the first page. It was all she needed to get the abortion she had thought she wanted. She wiped viciously at the tears that streaked her face, then ripped the sheet off the stack of papers and rumpled it, turning it over and over in her fist until it shrank to the size of a golf ball.

She continued to finger the paper ball when she entered the dorm lobby a few minutes later. Absently she walked down a wide hall away from the elevator and into one of the small doorless visiting rooms that lined both sides of the walkway. She dropped the paper into an ashtray on the table and lit a match, setting it to the paper ball. She watched as it burned, tears still flooding her cheeks.

Later, in her room, she searched for a tissue. She rifled through her purse, spilling its contents out onto her desk. Her wallet fell open and there in a clear plastic picture slot was the business card Reverend Callahan had given her. "Call me," he'd said, then watched her put the card into her purse. She hesitated for a moment, then picked up the phone's receiver and dialed the number.

"Reverend Callahan," she heard from the other end of the line.

"Hello," she began weakly. "This is Cybil Renwick, we talked at the health center a couple of days ago."

"Yes, how are you?"

"Not so great, Reverend." Cybil heard the soft thud of a

book closing, then the minister's voice came more clearly across the line as if he'd turned his mouth closer to the receiver.

"What can I do for you, Cybil?"

"My parents . . . they're not going to help." There was a brief pause and she heard the minister clear his throat before he responded.

"Then I'll help; I'm really very good at it, Cybil, if you'll forgive my pride. If you've decided to have the abortion, I can only —"

Cybil leaned back in her chair and tried to rub the ache from behind her eyes. "No! I can't do that."

"Good." His voice was quiet and sweet. "I'd have held your hand after it was over, but that wouldn't have been much help. I'm glad for your decision."

"So am I, thank you," she whispered.

"Well, let's see where to begin. You're near the end of a term at school, aren't you?"

"Yes."

"Then you'll want to finish it out. That won't be too difficult, will it?"

"No. I can manage that." Cybil swallowed hard and leaned forward, picking up a small ceramic figurine from the desk in front of her. The statuette was a skier, her comical face screwed up with fear and her skis crossed in front. "It's all downhill from here" was inscribed on the base below. Cybil smiled in spite of herself.

"After that you'll need a place to stay. Have you other relatives? We can make other arrangements for you if you don't."

"No, I mean, yes, but I don't want that. At least not yet. I can fit in another quarter of school before the baby comes."

"Good. Now you're thinking clearly. Tell me what you want to do and we'll see how I can help."

"Spring break's in April. I'll leave school then and . . . I don't know . . . I have an aunt in California. She owns a preschool. I've worked for her before in the summertime."

"Would you be welcome there?"

"I think so."

"Call her now, so she can plan on your visit, and tell her everything."

"That'll be hard."

"Not as hard as telling your parents—you've handled the worst part. The rest is all downhill."

Cybil kissed the head of the figurine still in her hand and laughed to herself. "You're right, Reverend. Thanks."

"Cybil?"

"Yes?"

"Call your parents and tell them what you've decided. I know they've hurt you, but they'll need to know. Can you do that?"

"Yes," she said shakily.

"I have your phone number from your file at the center. Do you mind if I use it from time to time? I promise not to bug you, but I'd like to check back with you."

"Sure."

"And, Cybil, call me when you need to—anytime."

Cybil's throat closed off until she had to swallow hard to answer. When she did, her voice was weak and tear-filled. "Thank you," was all she could say.

"We never meant to say you weren't wanted here." Cybil's mother sounded tired, and Cybil knew she was sincere. Her anger dissipated and she felt relieved. *They love me*, she thought. *Be fair.*

"I know, Mom," she said. She wished she could put her arms around her mother. "Dad's right. This'll be hard for everybody if I stay there."

"But where will you go?"

Cybil wondered if her mother was relieved. She was certain her father would be.

"Aunt Cora's," she finally said. "I've already talked to her, and she says to come ahead."

So it was decided. She would drive to California as soon as her second quarter was finished.

Twenty-Three

Cybil didn't know why her pregnancy had changed her feelings toward Mike, but it had. It was a normal reaction, she supposed.

She hoped her condition wouldn't be obvious before spring break. Unfortunately, she was not so lucky. Her narrow waistline seemed to broaden almost immediately along with her hips. By the first week in April, her tummy had become round and full, and none of her clothes fit. Julie had remained absolutely faithful in keeping her secret, and she had helped in other ways to allay people's suspicions. ("Too much eggnog, too many cookies," she crooned.) But there was only so much that could be done.

Cybil avoided Michael. She knew his class schedule and all his favorite hangouts. It hadn't been difficult, but a meeting with Mike was inevitable.

One day when the elevator doors opened, Mike was waiting across the foyer looking straight into the cubicle. The sight of him took her breath away. All the reasons she had been so desperate to please him returned to her memory.

"Hi," he said. "Long time no see."

The spring day had been sunny, but the air was damp, and Cybil pulled her jacket closed as they stepped outside. They drove to a quiet spot on campus where they could sit and talk undisturbed. She waited until he spoke.

"Why didn't you tell me?" he asked.

"Tell you what?"

"C'mon, Cybil. You're pregnant. Didn't you think I should know?"

"What makes you so sure the baby's yours?"

"Don't give me that." He looked at her. She did not look directly at him, but she was aware of every movement. He sighed, "I know you—I think—pretty well, and I know there weren't any other guys—before, during, or since me."

Cybil was touched by his regard for her. She didn't answer.

"Why? Cybil . . . why didn't you tell me?"

Cybil stifled tears and remained silent.

"Talk to me. Please!"

"I was afraid."

"Afraid of me? What have I ever done to make you afraid—"

She interrupted him. "No, not like that. I was afraid you'd pressure me to get an abortion."

"Well, that's not a bad idea."

"Then I was right not to tell you."

"You could still get one, you know. I've asked around. No one would ever need to know about this. It'd be better for both of us."

She couldn't believe it. *Both* of us. But there was a third person concerned that everyone seemed to be forgetting.

Mike continued. "Abortions are legal. It'd only take a few minutes to—"

"No!" She stood abruptly and walked away.

"Wait a minute!" He walked after her, his long legs covering the same distance in half the time. He took her arm. "I don't think I'm being unreasonable. It would simplify both our lives. Look, I've still got school, you've still got—"

She could argue with him, but she didn't want a fight. "Both our lives? There's another person involved in this, you know. A helpless little . . . "

He blustered. "Wha . . . You've got to be kidding."

"Well, you're really feeling smug, aren't you? I'm not kidding," she said.

"All right. All right! What are you going to do with a baby?"

Cybil was disappointed that he hadn't called it his baby or their baby. He obviously had no such feelings.

"I didn't get an abortion because it's wrong. I've decided to give the baby up for adoption."

"Then you're not going to keep it."

"No."

"Well, thank goodness for that!"

His attitude surprised her, and it hurt. "Well, thank goodness for your approval," she mocked him.

"Listen, Cybil, don't be that way with me. I can't quit school. I don't have a job. I have a career to build. If you'd asked me you'd have ended the whole problem long ago. I'm sorry. I just can't get married now."

"You know, Mike, you really don't know what you're saying. And I wouldn't marry you if you were the last man in the world!" She began to walk away again. She'd walk back to the dorm in the dark before she'd listen to his mindless selfishness.

He stopped her again. "Meaning?"

"Meaning—I don't need you. I'll get through this by myself."

"C'mon Cybil. Get real! That . . . " He gestured toward her rounded middle. "It's not human until it's born."

"That's not true! Don't touch me. Just get away, leave me alone."

As she finished speaking she felt the baby move. It was a feeling she'd enjoyed for nearly a month, and the movement was getting stronger. It was strange thinking of herself as somebody's mother. She felt her abdomen and tried to imagine an infant stretching its tiny legs. Having Mike there enhanced the feeling, and she felt warmed by it. When the movement seemed certain to continue she took Mike's hand and placed it against her body so he could feel it, too. He allowed her to do so only a moment, then he pulled his hand away.

"I know you have no feelings for this baby. I guess I don't blame you. But he is yours as surely as he is mine." She turned to walk away from him again as she added the last of it. "And you would kill him merely to save us embarrassment."

Mike followed after her again and insisted that he take her back to the dorm. He said nothing as they drove. But before he helped her out of the car he said simply, "I'm sorry . . . for everything. Whatever you need . . . well, let me know. Okay?"

"Okay."

"I mean it."

"I know you do."

Twenty-Four

It pleased Jeff to find Maggie's car in the garage when he arrived home from school one day in June after a full day of teaching. It had been warm, but evenings on the beach were always breezy and cool. Jeff pulled his sweater on over his head as he stepped out of the car. _One more week of classes, then finals, and I'll be done for the summer_ Jeff thought, lifting a stack of papers off the back seat. His rock group was already booked solid through September, so he'd be busy nights, but he looked forward to sleeping in and spending his days with Maggie at home. His dual career meant they couldn't get away in the summer as their teaching colleagues did, but their both having the summer off meant more time together. That was especially important this year after their blowup in Norfolk.

The radio played louder than usual as he approached their front door. "Maggie?" he called as he stepped across the threshold. When she didn't answer he went looking for her. He didn't have to go far.

He laughed out loud when he saw what she was doing. Maggie had the doors of the deep closet opposite their bedroom wide open. A fan inside brought her a constant supply of fresh air, and she was lying face down, her entire upper body buried inside.

The scene amused Jeff, and he stood there for a moment watching. He crouched near the opening and called again, "Maggie."

She didn't answer. With the radio blaring and the noise of the fan, she obviously couldn't hear.

The muscles in Maggie's shapely derriere tightened suddenly, as she apparently stretched toward something just out of reach. Jeff watched with interest and, smiling mischievously, ran playful fingers across its fullness.

She jumped, and he heard a muffled thud, then . . .

"Ouch! Jeff?" She pushed herself backwards out of the closet.

"It'd better be me. I'm sorry," he added through his laughter as she sat up in front of him, rubbing her head. He kissed her. "You're a good sport."

She returned the kiss and smiled.

Jeff was glad to see it. These days Maggie seemed to smile all the time. It had been six months since they'd decided to adopt a baby—a painful decision through which Jeff had carefully avoided forcing his point of view. They'd spent the week after Norfolk talking about the problems with their relationship. But they avoided the subject that concerned them most until the end of that week.

Maggie wanted their own baby, of course. That's what he wanted, too, but he found that dream easier to give up than she did. Their talks had resolved a lot of conflict between them, but the important thing remained undecided.

On Sunday afternoon Jeff sat at the piano playing from the opening movement of Mozart's Piano Concerto number 20 in D Minor. The somber melody reflected his mood, and he poured his soul into it. He felt Maggie's arms rest on his shoulders and her body press against him. She waited until he finished, then she said, "Beautiful, Jeff. Mozart?"

"Yes."

She moved away from him, trailing her fingers across his back, and sat on the piano bench next to him. She rested her head against his shoulder without speaking.

"Maggie, we've got to make a decision," he said after enjoying her closeness for a long moment.

"I know."

"I don't know how we'll afford it, but if you want to try the *in vitro* process again, we'll work it out."

"No." Maggie tucked her arm under his and took his left hand in both hers. She gently rubbed her cheek against his shoulder.

"Are you sure?" He pulled away from her and turned to face her squarely.

Maggie clung to his hand and watched his fingers tighten around hers. "Yes. I'm tired of disappointments. Adoption's a sure thing. That's what I want—a sure thing."

The next day Maggie had gone to LDS Social Services after getting advice from a lawyer, and had filled out the preliminary forms. Since then they had attended meetings, had been interviewed together and separately, and had filled out even more forms. And they'd prayed about it—constantly. Every new question, every new form, brought new concerns and another need for answers. In the end, the agency had informed them that their application had been provisionally accepted. All that was left was a home visit to determine finally if they could provide a suitable environment for a child.

"What's all this?" Jeff couldn't believe Maggie's diligence in preparing for the agency's home visit. She had spent all week scrubbing, drying, organizing, polishing every forgotten spot in their small home.

"Do you really think anyone is going to look in that closet?"

"I'm not taking any chances. By the end of today, everything in this house will be spotless. Monday morning all I'll have to do is last-minute straightening, dusting, and vacuuming one more time, and I'll be ready." She paused. "Tell me again it's all going to be okay," she pleaded.

Jeff shook his head, chuckling to himself. "You get this place too clean and they're going to think we're too antiseptic."

Maggie's chin dropped and her eyes widened. One look at her face made him laugh out loud. "Maggie . . . I'm kidding. C'mon. We're a sure win," he said. "Anyway, you're carrying this too far and I won't have it." He took her hand and led her into the bathroom, where he directed her to relax in a hot tub while he finished what she'd started.

"We're going out this evening with friends."

"Who?"

"I have tickets to that new play at the Dorothy Chandler Pavilion."

"Jeff. Who are we going with?"

"Darn, Mag, it was supposed to be a surprise. Gretchen and Carl are here. They're on their way to San Diego and stopped off for the weekend."

"Gretchen?" Maggie yelped. "Why didn't you call me? Why didn't *they* call me?" Maggie followed him around the living room as he picked up litter from the closet and shoved boxes of books and music back through its opening.

"They tried. I tried—several times. Your line's been busy."

"Oh, yeah. I took it off the hook. I kept getting interrupted, and I have so much to do . . . they're going to stay with us overnight, I hope."

"They're here *without* their *six* kids, Maggie. I don't think sleeping on our couch is what they had in mind. They've already checked into the Ramada down the street. C'mon, get moving. We're picking them up in an hour."

"Wow!" Jeff said as they met Gretchen and Carl in the hotel lobby. "You Barnett sisters are going to set the town on fire tonight." He and Carl stood back and admired their wives collectively as the two women exchanged warm hugs.

"Keep talking, boy," Gretchen responded as she took Jeff's hand and as Maggie kissed Carl on the cheek. "Are we dressed to kill, or what?" Both women were dressed in long formals, Gretchen's a green silk shirtwaist with rhinestones studding the collar and cuffs, and Maggie's a deep purple crepe that hung loosely from the shoulders across her long shapely form. The men wore black-tie attire.

Once at the theatre, Jeff handed the usher their tickets as Gretchen admired the enormous chandeliers that lined the ceiling of the pavilion's elegant foyer. The crescent-shaped anteroom filled quickly as people of all types poured in through the several entrances. People were dressed in everything from casual sports clothes to mink-trimmed opulence. One woman wore what looked like a swimsuit under a long sequin-studded sheer lace overdress. Jeff caught himself staring when Gretchen leaned toward him and said, "If the play is half as entertaining as this show, we'll have a great evening." They all laughed.

The comedy was just the right diversion. It kept their minds off the adoption—just what they needed—until later, at the restaurant, the conversation turned. Jeff couldn't remember who asked the first question or made the first comment. He regretted it, but he supposed it was inevitable.

"How's it going?" Carl asked.

"The caseworker is coming for a home visit Monday afternoon."

Gretchen looked surprised. "I knew that was coming up, but I didn't know it was so soon." Then, pulling a dread-filled face, she continued, "I'll bet you've been cleaning everything in sight."

Maggie jumped on the comment and turned to Jeff. "See, Gretchen knows. Jeff thinks I'm crazy for worrying so much about it," she added.

"Gretchen, she has taken everything out of every drawer, cupboard, and closet in the house. We've taken truckloads to the Deseret Industries. If we hadn't just repainted, I think she'd have me doing that, too. And all of this on top of preparing for her Primary leadership meeting. She's been dead on her feet."

"She'll survive it, and I don't blame her." Gretchen smiled. "Let me give you another hint from a friend of mine. Carl's secretary has adopted four children, and she swears this little detail makes the difference on the home visits."

Maggie listened eagerly as Jeff cast his eyes up to the ceiling in disbelief.

Gretchen took mock offense at Jeff's attitude. "This is serious business, Jeff," she said. "You have to know the tricks." Turning her attention back to Maggie and with posture bent in total seriousness she said, "You bake bread."

"What?" Jeff asked.

"Now wait a minute. It makes sense to me . . . I think," Maggie responded.

"Of course it makes sense. Look, what makes you think of home and Mom and warm kitchens sooner than the smell of something lovin' coming from the oven?" She sat back and waited. "Huh? Am I right?"

Jeff and Carl looked at each other. Both shook with laughter.

"I'm serious. You mix up a batch of homemade bread in the morning, at just the right time, so it'll be ready to come out of the oven a minute or two before the agency woman comes. According to my friend, timing is very important. You don't want to have your visit with her interrupted by anything. But you want the house still full of that wonderful aroma when she arrives."

"What if she doesn't come on time?" Maggie asked.

"Oh, she'll be prompt. Those people always are."

"Maggie, Gretchen's kidding," Jeff said.

Maggie was wide-eyed as she looked first at Jeff and then at her sister. "No, she isn't," she replied.

"No, I'm not. Listen, Jeff, you're an artist. You know that we're all influenced by whatever touches our senses. What we feel about everything is colored by what we see, hear, smell, and touch."

Maggie thought about it for a minute, then said, "I'll do it."

"You're going to bake bread the same morning you do last-minute straightening, vacuuming, dusting, and, I expect, floor mopping?" he asked. "She's worn the no-wax shine off the kitchen floor."

"That's not true. I don't know why you're so smug anyway." Maggie began counting on her fingers. "In the last week he's cleaned the garage, hand-waxed the car, hosed down the outside of the house including the patio fence which the woman will never see, swept the walk clear to the street, picked up debris off the beach for a block in both directions, and gotten a haircut and a manicure. Now you tell me he's not concerned."

By the time Maggie finished her list, Carl and Gretchen were laughing hysterically. "Well." Carl's voice hit a high-pitched squeak as he tried to control his laughter. He cleared his throat and continued, "At least she'll know you're serious about wanting a child. None of it can hurt."

Jeff, who could still feel the blush on his face, relaxed back in his seat and said, "Yeah, can't hurt."

Jeff reflected on how they had changed their lives to get the baby they wanted. Trying to favorably impress the agency people was merely the most recent part of it.

"I just hope whoever the agency sends is sympathetic." Knowing that that wasn't the word he wanted, he shrugged with frustration. No word could describe what they wanted from the caseworker whose recommendation was of primary importance to them. Maybe home-baked bread wasn't such a bad idea; it couldn't hurt.

Dr. Barnett's obstetrical practice offered him opportunities to arrange adoptions for people he knew were looking for a baby. The new abortion ruling had reduced the number of single pregnant women he treated but hadn't eliminated it. He'd called a month ago and told Maggie he had such a patient who wished to have a hand in selecting parents for her child. He suggested they apply.

Maggie was ecstatic. It meant eliminating the long wait that going through the agency would entail. He quickly added that the mother was going to choose from several couples, so there were no guarantees, but they would be in the running.

Maggie began that evening to write their resume. She made a note to herself to call the social worker who had taken their case, so they could get a copy of her report sent to the lawyer. The necessary paperwork was taken care of within a couple of days and was sent off by certified mail.

The waiting after was unbearable.

Then a letter came from the lawyer handling their case. Maggie opened it while Jeff was out. She was shocked at first. What he proposed seemed terribly irregular. The biological mother of the baby she wanted so badly wanted to meet them. Maggie didn't like the idea.

"Oh, Jeff. I'm glad you're home," she said the minute he came in. "We got a letter from Mr. Trenton."

"What? No 'hello, how are you?' " He leaned down to kiss her. She responded, then handed him the well-read document.

He smiled as he took the letter.

"Well, what do you think?" Maggie asked before he could finish it.

"Honey, give me a chance," he insisted as he read it a second time. "I don't know, Maggie. It seems kind of risky. If she knows who we are, she could make life miserable for us after the adoption."

"Not if it's all legally done. Dad's the girl's doctor. He says she's not the flaky type. Jeff, please don't say no without thinking about it!"

Jeff cringed, knowing how he deserved that. "I'm trying, Maggie."

"I know, I'm sorry. I'm going to call Dad," Maggie said. "He knows the girl; he'll have a better sense of what she wants from this."

Jeff picked up the extension phone.

The summer day had been hot and Maggie had opened all the windows facing the ocean. A cooling breeze soothed them as they waited for her father's answer.

"Maggie, she's a sensible girl who's done a lot of growing up in a very short time," Dr. Barnett began. "She doesn't want to keep the baby. I don't think you need to worry about her changing her mind."

"You don't *think*, Dad. Is that good enough?"

"There are no guarantees. You know that. This open adoption idea is new, but from what I've read it's worked out well for lots of people."

"I don't want to meet her. Why can't it be done the other way and avoid all this worry over it?"

"You're not seeing it from the mother's side. She doesn't want to rely on other people's judgment concerning the choice of parents for her child. You should be able to understand that."

"No, Dad. I don't understand. Why would a girl like that care—so long as she is freed of the responsibility?"

"Maggie, you're being unfairly cruel."

"I know. I'm sorry, but I can't understand anyone who'd give up a baby."

Jeff felt the pathos behind his wife's reasoning. He heard her pull the piano bench out and sit down on it. A few of the keys sounded as she leaned against them. The keyboard cover closed with a thud. He could picture her resting her head and shoulders on the smooth, cool surface. He sat down on the edge of their bed and stifled a sigh. Maggie was in charge of publicity for a stake Primary meeting, and large, brightly colored posters leaned against the walls of their bedroom. Pictures of children doing everything from praying to playing hopscotch covered them. *Children*, Jeff thought. The happy little faces warmed him and brought tears to his eyes. The door to the garage at the end of the hall was open, and the rhythmic sound of the washing machine swishing back and forth lulled him. He stretched out on the bed and wiped his face against his shoulder, the telephone receiver still pressed to his ear.

"Just take my word for it," his father-in-law continued. "She cares. And open adoptions have advantages for both sides. The mother agrees to send on medical information about herself that might be important to the development of the child. The adoptive parents send the mother pictures occasionally . . . that sort of thing. Legal limits to the amount of contact with the natural mother can, of course, be clearly defined."

There was a pause without response. Jeff picked up his phone in the bedroom and carried it into the hall, where he could see Maggie. She rubbed her thumb and forefinger into her eye sockets, tension apparent on her face. He leaned back against the door frame and spoke next in her place.

"Dad, what do you think?" he asked. "Would you do it? Would you meet with her?"

"Yes, I think I would, Jeff. Is Maggie still listening?"

"Yes. This is hard for her," Jeff responded.

"I'm sure it is. Look, sweetheart, I know this is a tough decision for you and Jeff to make, but you're not legally committed until you sign those papers. It seems to me that anything up to that point is worth the risk."

"I'd feel like a mongrel pup in the pound," Maggie replied, "wagging my tail and doing my tricks just so some stupid kid in trouble would pick me."

"What do you say, Jeff?" Dr. Barnett asked.

"Maggie and I need to talk about it. We'll get back to you."

When they said goodbye to her father Maggie went directly into Jeff's arms. They held each other tightly. After a moment Jeff released her and, still holding her hands, he leaned back against the door frame again and pulled Maggie close to him. This time her eyes met his at the same level. They would talk.

"What do you think?"

Maggie watched him closely. "I want to know what you think," she responded.

"Okay. I say we go for it."

Maggie sat up straight and unlatched her seat belt the moment the jet came to a stop. She pulled a mirror from her purse and looked critically at her makeup. She ran a comb through her hair, frowned, sighed, and shoved the mirror back in her purse. Jeff watched her, smiling. He munched silently on some jelly beans. He sorted through the bag, pushing the licorice aside and picking up the fruit flavors. Maggie had gone through torture that morning deciding what to wear. It reminded him of the week she had spent cleaning house before the social worker's visit. Her skirt had been pressed twice, once with a steam iron and again with spray starch. He could still smell the fresh, warm scent of the heated cotton fabric. She'd tried three or four different pairs of earrings and a half dozen scarves, only to decide against all of them. Even when she appeared to be satisfied she had to turn to him for confirmation. "You look great," he'd said. Now it looked as if she was going to start all over again.

Jeff leaned her way and said, "You look great. Have a jelly bean. The red ones are good, but I'd stay away from the black ones."

She looked surprised, then smiled. A few minutes later she had the mirror out again. He shrugged silently and ate another jelly bean.

Dr. Barnett was to meet them at the airport. People crowded through the narrow tunnel to the terminal, and even more people waited there. Several minutes passed before Maggie and Jeff saw him. He wore a heavy overcoat, and Jeff wondered if they were going to be sorry they hadn't brought warmer clothing.

"Dad," Maggie said as she embraced him.

"How are you doing?" he asked.

"We're fine, honestly fine." Jeff extended his hand.

The older man took his son-in-law's hand and said, "Jeff." Looking them both over, he added, "Well, you look fine. Any luggage?"

"No, just this." Jeff had a small overnighter in his other hand. "And a bag of jelly beans. We travel light." He patted his pocket.

Dr. Barnett smiled.

Maggie pulled her sweater closed around her as they stepped outside. The airport, situated on the inside of the bay, was often foggy, and though it was now summertime, it was cool. Jeff wrapped his free arm around her shoulder and she snuggled close to him. As they walked to the parking lot Maggie asked, "How are the meetings going with the mother?"

"There are only three couples, including you, still involved. She met with one yesterday, and I haven't talked to her since." Dr. Barnett pulled his keys from his pocket and directed them to a parking aisle to their left.

"I don't mind telling you, Dad, I don't like being picked from a lineup like this. And especially by a girl with obviously questionable judgment."

"I know it's rough, honey, but you're wrong about Cybil. She's a very levelheaded girl. She's also commented that the selection process didn't seem right, somehow. But this is pretty much what happens when an agency makes their choices. They consider all the candidates and investigate them thoroughly. There's nothing immoral about it; it just has to be done."

"Does the girl know I'm your daughter?"

156

"No, not yet."

"Why not?"

"Maggie, for heaven's sake!" Jeff interrupted. "Be fair."

"I'm trying to, but I *want* this, and . . . "

"Jeff's right." Dr. Barnett gave his daughter an understanding hug. "We're treading a legal tightrope here. We have to be absolutely fair to the girl—no pressure at all. Otherwise, the whole deal could turn bad on us."

"I know that, Dad, but surely knowing who we are wouldn't do that."

Dr. Barnett stopped walking, took his daughter's hands in his, and faced her squarely. "Maggie, listen to me and understand," he began. "I love you and Jeff and want you to have this baby as badly as anybody, but I have an obligation to this girl who is my patient. I'll not put pressure on her, because to do so would be immoral; and that's an attitude completely separate from the legal requirements of this case. And, yes, I think her knowing who you are will affect her decision. I've kept that fact from her as long as I could. It was simple when we were dealing with names on paperwork. Unfortunately that changed when the girl asked to meet you. I haven't known what to do about it, so I've just waited." He released Maggie's hands and began walking again. "I've thought it through a dozen times since then, and I believe she'll have to know now. I'll see her first and tell her before you meet her."

_____ *Twenty-Five*

Cybil arrived early, hoping to be there first. The meeting the day before had been awkward because the couple was there waiting for her. She had felt strangely on display and very alone when she walked into the lawyer's office.

This time, when she saw Dr. Barnett waiting for her, she was relieved. She had become secure in his friendship.

"Hello, Cybil." He put an arm around her shoulders. "How'd the visit go yesterday?"

"It was okay, I guess. I suppose I want a bolt of lightning or something to say, '*These are the ones.*' " She paused for a moment. "I know that's not going to happen . . . this may all be wasted."

"It's not wasted if it makes you feel better about your choice."

Cybil put an arm around his waist and hugged him. "Are they here yet? . . . the Perrys?"

"Yes. Mr. Trenton is busy in his office with another client." Dr. Barnett looked at his watch. "We're a little early. The Perrys are in the conference room." He gestured toward the door.

"Do we have to wait for Mr. Trenton?"

"I think that would be wise, Cybil. He's your lawyer — for your protection."

"I know, but —"

The secretary interrupted her. "Mr. Trenton said to go on in. He'll be tied up for a while. He'll be in as soon as he can."

Dr. Barnett shrugged and then nodded his head, but stopped Cybil with a touch as she started toward the door.

"I have something I must tell you about this couple before you meet them."

He hesitated long enough to make Cybil wonder what could be wrong with them. She hoped it wasn't something major; this scene was heavy enough.

"No, no. Nothing terrible," he said, then paused before he spoke again. "The woman is my daughter. I didn't tell you before because I didn't want to bias your choice in their favor. If I had stayed out of it, I suppose we might have kept the secret. As it is, you'd have figured it out, probably fairly quickly."

She said nothing. He opened the door for her and then followed her into the room. The room was long and narrow, with a table in the center and chairs arranged all around it. One wall was paneled with dark wood and the rest were papered with a simple coarse-weave design in a soft gold color. A room-sized oriental rug adorned the hardwood floor. The young couple had pulled their chairs away from the table and were sitting next to each other against a side wall.

Jeff stood as soon as the door opened. He'd been holding his wife's hand. When he stood, he didn't release it until he'd reached almost his full height. The awkward movement made the tender gesture obvious to Cybil. She smiled.

"Cybil, I'd like you to meet my daughter, Maggie, and her husband, Jeff Perry. Maggie and Jeff, this is Cybil Renwick."

Cybil shook both their hands in turn.

Jeff was the first to speak. "I'm sure this is as awkward for you as it is for us, Miss Renwick. But where do we begin?"

Cybil sat in a chair Dr. Barnett had pulled forward for her. The others followed. She felt fat and uncomfortably warm, and she silently agreed that this was, indeed, awkward. "I don't know. Suppose we just talk," she suggested.

She watched carefully as Jeff nervously shifted position, leaning forward with elbows on his knees. Maggie gently put her hand on his leg. He acknowledged the gesture of comfort with a smile.

Then, turning attention back to Cybil, Maggie said, "It's hard to know what to say, Miss Renwick. We're happy to be here — now. To be truthful, we had some misgivings about this at first, but now that we're here" — she looked back at Jeff momentarily, then continued — "we're glad to meet you."

"Did you have a nice flight?" Cybil asked, regretting it immediately. Cybil twisted awkwardly sideways in her chair and rested her hands atop her swollen middle. She looked up to see Maggie staring strangely at her. *I wonder what she's thinking?*

"Yes. Very nice, thank you," Jeff answered quickly, and Maggie agreed.

"Actually we make this trip quite often to visit Maggie's folks," Jeff continued. Cybil felt he would have said more if he hadn't been stopped by the lawyer's entering the room. Jeff stood to greet him as Dr. Barnett introduced him and Maggie.

"Well, how are you getting along?"

"As fine as can be expected," Dr. Barnett responded.

"That's typically medical." Mr. Trenton laughed.

They all laughed, but the moment was followed by another awkward silence.

Mr. Trenton began immediately with the business at hand. He was obviously anxious that the Perrys understand the legal ramifications of an *open adoption*. Since that was what they had, he explained, there was no point in considering any further until all agreed to that arrangement.

The meeting went on for more than an hour, during which every aspect of the adoption agreement was discussed. Jeff commented that the discussion was a little premature, as it seemed to presuppose that they would be the adoptive parents. But the lawyer explained that Cybil had wanted it that way. Knowing how the couples felt about the unique arrangement could have a bearing on her final decision.

"I'm not sure I understand the reason for our sending Miss Renwick pictures. I really don't see what good that will do." Maggie spoke directly to Mr. Trenton.

"Honey, it's a fair exchange for the medical information she would promise us. I don't see any harm in it." Jeff looked at Cybil when he finished. She'd been watching them but looked away.

"It seems to me that that arrangement would just encourage unseemly interest from her. Why torture herself?"

"That's not for us to decide."

"Jeff, I think you're wrong. We have a lot at stake here, and . . . "

"Excuse us," Jeff said as he looked around and noted everyone's eyes on them. He stood, took Maggie's hand, and directed her to the far corner of the room.

Cybil watched them with interest. She wished she could hear what they said, but even without that, a message came through.

Jeff spoke first. He squared off opposite his wife and offered his opinion in obvious, deliberate tones. Cybil liked the way they looked at each other as they talked. At one point Cybil saw him gently touch Maggie's cheek with the back side of one finger. It wasn't until he reached for his handkerchief that the girl realized he'd wiped a tear away.

When he finished speaking he relaxed his posture, stuffed his hands in his pockets, and watched his wife's face closely as she spoke. He started to interrupt at one point but backed off when Maggie objected. When Maggie finished she pulled a chair away from the table and sat down. Jeff stepped to the window and looked out. He ran the fingers of both hands back through his hair, took a deep breath, then relaxed and put his hands back in his pockets. After a moment Maggie joined him at the window. They talked some more. Finally, Jeff kissed his wife discreetly, then directed her back to their chairs next to the others. They'd apparently agreed. Cybil wasn't sure who had won, but it had all been sweetly done. She was impressed. How different her childhood would have been if her parents had been able to do as well.

"I read somewhere in your file that you're Mormons," Cybil commented the instant the couple rejoined the group. The statement broke an awkward silence and changed the subject abruptly. It came out sounding cold. Cybil was sorry for that.

The Perrys looked at each other, then at Dr. Barnett and Mr. Trenton and back to Cybil. "I'm sorry," she continued. "I'm not religious myself, but it seems to me the question is relevant. I don't know much about it — I mean, I've heard rumors. I'd like to know what your religion will mean to the baby — the child — growing up."

"Of course." Jeff's voice cracked and he stopped to clear his throat. He began again, speaking slowly and measuring every word carefully. "Actually, the Church philosophy toward children is very positive. We believe we're all children of a loving God who wants nothing but what's best for us — what'll make us happy. That includes good, moral living, of course, but not harsh living. Children are taught to obey rules, respect and honor their parents. But parents are also guided to teach with kindness and to follow necessary discipline with an 'increase of love.' We believe in life after death and in Christ as our Savior. Children are taught to choose the right so that they can be worthy to live with Him and the Father in the next life. We try to live a life dedicated to serving Christ and our fellowman. Maggie teaches a Primary class — that's the younger group's auxiliary — and I coach basketball for teenage boys. Most adults in the Church volunteer in one way or another to help the system run smoothly." Jeff had been talking directly to Cybil. He stopped and looked at Maggie, then back to Cybil again. "Does that help? If you have specific questions, perhaps . . ."

"Yes, that helps, thank you. Look, I don't want to make you uncomfortable and especially about something so personal as religion, but I have to know. There are no cultish activities, weird rituals? I'm sorry, but that's what I've heard."

"No," Dr. Barnett answered. "I'm a Latter-day Saint also, Cybil. We've reared all our children in the Church. I can get you some reading material if you'd like. What you've heard comes from our enemies and is not true at all. What Jeff has told you is the truth. Believe me, you can't do better than a Latter-day Saint home for your baby."

"I'll second that," added Mr. Trenton, "and I'm not a Mormon. But I have several friends who are."

Cybil felt relieved. She admired Dr. Barnett and had learned to trust him. She was sorry she'd made him defensive. She looked around at the others. The Perrys looked worried. She wanted to say something that would alleviate the fear she'd apparently raised in them. "I'm sorry if I've offended you. I'll be glad to read your literature . . . thank you."

"I don't suppose you know yet how it will go," Mrs. Barnett asked as she put sandwiches and glasses of milk on the table. By noon the day had turned warm, and a shimmering stream of sunlight filled the room from the kitchen's back windows. Jeff had changed into Levi's and a T-shirt and came down the back stairs. Maggie followed in a white jumpsuit and tennis shoes.

"No. We won't know for at least another week. The last interview is next Wednesday." Dr. Barnett took a seat at the table and Jeff sat next to him.

"I think she liked us, though, Mom." Maggie washed and cored apples at the sink. "But I don't understand her. She seems like a really nice girl and bright, too. How did she get herself into such a mess?" She put the sliced apples in a bowl and placed them in the center of the table before sitting down. "I mean . . . how does a nice, bright girl decide to give her baby away?"

Dr. Barnett frowned. "You need to learn a little compassion for other people's failings. Cybil knows she's made a terrible mistake. She's trying to correct it the best way she knows how."

"By giving her baby away?"

"Jeff, would you give thanks before we eat?" Dr. Barnett asked, his face still sporting a frown.

Jeff said a brief prayer, then waited while the rest began to eat. "Maggie," he said looking at her as she bit into her sandwich, "She must see adoption as the best thing for her child."

"I suppose. But I want that baby so badly, it's impossible for me to understand how she can give it away."

"Let's go for a walk and shake down the tuna fish," Jeff said to Maggie as they finished their lunch.

"I ought to stay and help Mother with the dishes."

Jeff took the dishes from Maggie's hands and put them on the counter next to the dishwasher. "I'll help you finish this when we get back. I've got to get out of the house. I'm turning into a couch potato. Tell her to come with me, Mom."

"Go along, Maggie. You can both have another piece of pie when you get back."

"Well, all right, but don't do these." Maggie quickly gathered up the glasses and set them next to the plates. "We'll do them, we promise."

They hadn't walked a block when Jeff challenged Maggie to a race.

"From here to the drugstore on First Avenue," he said.

"That must be at least a mile from here."

"Yeah. That's what I figured."

"No way."

"C'mon. Be a sport." He assumed a boxer's pose, poked her, then took off running. She ran after him. He loped along until she passed him, then he increased his speed just enough to keep up with her. When Maggie slumped onto the bus stop bench near the pharmacy she looked exhausted. Jeff wasn't even breathing hard.

"You make me sick, you know that?" She teasingly took a half dozen jabs at him. The last two or three caught him pretty squarely, and he moved to stop her. With his left hand he caught her right arm as it flew at him one last time and, turning behind her, he wrapped his right arm around her waist. He held her tightly until she stopped squirming.

"You know, Mag, a month of jogging with me in the morning and you'd be able to run that far—no sweat."

He stood again and began to run in place. "C'mon, jellyfish," he said. Let's jog around the park. It'd do you good."

"Forget it, Sam. Do your thing if that's what you want, but leave me be." She smiled up at him. "I'll be right here when you get back."

Cybil smiled inwardly as she watched the Perrys from her vantage point. The bench where they'd chosen to rest was beneath the kitchen window of the converted frame house that was now Aunt Cora's preschool. Cybil was just beginning to wash the lunch dishes when Jeff and Maggie ran panting to the bus stop bench. She watched closely and listened through the open window. She continued to observe them as Jeff ran off toward the park, and again as he came jogging back a few minutes later.

Maggie was sitting with her knees clutched to her chest, her heels hooked to the front edge of the bench, and her toes pointing down over it. She was so deeply in thought, her face pressed against her knees, that she wasn't aware of Jeff when he eased himself down at the other end of the long wooden seat. He sat for a few seconds with legs sprawled in front of him and fingers drumming against the wooden plank between his legs. After a few seconds, he sat up and leaned toward her.

"Are you all right?" he asked.

"Oh, Jeff," she answered, startled. "I'm . . . okay, I guess." She remained silent a moment longer, then she asked, "What happens if we don't get this baby?"

Cybil saw the young husband run tense fingers back through his hair before he answered. He relaxed and then spoke. "We wait for a while and get a different one," he said.

Cybil knew he was right. They would have their baby eventually. They needed only be patient. But she had been impatient at times — in fact, often — when she wanted things; and those were just things. She had no trouble understanding how this young woman felt who wanted a baby so badly. She continued to watch. The young woman dipped her face into her lap again, and her husband put an arm warmly around her.

"It's going to be fine, kid." He had stretched his legs out in front of him again and had taken on a kind of macho attitude. That, combined with his not-too-bad impression of Bogart, made the pose quite funny. Maggie laughed and turned her head into his shoulder. He turned to face her and kissed the top of her curls. She melted at his tenderness and wrapped her arms around his chest.

Cybil had not missed a single nuance of feeling that had flowed between them. She was conscious of her sympathies turning in favor of this couple. It wasn't fair that the others had not had the same opportunity to impress her, but she wasn't concerned with fairness. She just wanted to be sure her baby had parents who would love him, and Jeff and Maggie Perry would love him.

Twenty-Six

"Maggie-o! Hand out the confetti, chill the oysters, and lay 'em on me!"

A TV producer had offered Jeff a part in a TV miniseries that was to air next spring. Jeff and Maggie had read the script; it was a good part. The meeting had gone well; they'd been able to agree on everything, and the contracts had been signed. Jeff was excited about sharing that news with Maggie. He'd brought the contracts, a dozen long-stemmed roses, and a three-layer box of hand-dipped chocolates.

"It's done," he said holding up the papers, the flowers, and the candy when he first saw her.

"That's terrific," Maggie responded, putting arms tightly around him. "Mmmm, I'm so proud of you," she said after kissing him. "Who wouldn't want you for their old movie. You'll have all the ladies drooling."

Jeff laughed. "You might be a little biased," he said. "Have a chocolate, on me."

"Maybe, but that doesn't make it any less true." She backed away from him. "Let me get a vase for these. Don't go away!"

"Fat chance. Did you just get home?" He noticed she was still dressed from her morning of shopping. "Let's go someplace exotic and expensive."

"I was just going to change. What did you have in mind?"

"How about Tijuana Tilly's?"

"Well . . . that's exotic, anyway."

"Have you checked for messages?" Jeff knew better than to ask. Maggie hated the recording machine that sat under the phone on the desk. He pushed the rewind button before she had a chance to answer. When it reached its end he punched the "play" key and turned up the volume so Maggie could hear it from the kitchen.

"This is your dad, Maggie. Call me back ASAP."

"You want to call, or shall I?" Jeff asked. Before Maggie could answer the second message began.

"It's me again. I need to talk to you—soon—Maggie or Jeff, I don't care."

"I wonder what he wan—" Jeff's question was interrupted by the machine again.

"Sorry, kids, to bother you again. It's lunchtime. I hoped Jeff would be there."

The last message sounded impatient. "Where've you been all morning, Jeff? When do you sleep? Anyway, I won't try again. Call me back when you can."

The machine whirred to a stop. Maggie stood in the doorway, clutching the vase in one hand, the roses in the other. They stared at each other, mouths gaping, for a long moment before she quickly put the vase and the flowers on the table and she and Jeff simultaneously reached for the phone. Jeff deferred to his wife, who dialed her parents' number. Jeff was beginning to wonder silently if anyone was home, when Mrs. Barnett answered.

"Mom? What's going on there?" Maggie asked . . . "I know. Is he there?"

Maggie looked toward Jeff and nodded, then turned her attention back toward the phone.

"I'm not going anywhere." Looking at Jeff, who was standing very close by, she added, "Dad just got home, she's getting him."

Jeff went into the bedroom and picked up the extension phone.

"Dad?" he heard Maggie question as he began to listen in. "Is there something wrong?"

"Hello, Margaret Ann," her father answered. "No . . . no, nothing wrong. In fact, everything's about as right as it could be."

Jeff didn't dare guess what that meant. There was a brief pause as he heard his father-in-law take a deep breath.

"You'll have your baby."

"The baby's ours?"

"Yes."

Jeff put the receiver back onto its cradle and returned to the living room, where he dropped into the large swivel chair. Still holding the phone, Maggie sat unceremoniously on his left knee and tightened her right arm around his neck. For a few moments they wept silently. Then Maggie leaned the receiver sideways between them so Jeff could hear her father.

"Tell Jeff that I never want to hear his voice again on one of those record-a-call things," Dr. Barnett insisted.

"When do we come to get the baby?"

"I'll notify you when he's born. You can come and get him as soon as he's ready to leave the hospital. There'll still be legalities to handle, but they won't keep you from having him right away."

"Just give us the word!"

Maggie was still on Jeff's lap, her entire body cradled in his left arm. Jeff hung up the receiver, then put his right hand around her knees and pulled her closer to him. He gave the chair a little spin as they hugged each other and smiled through their tears at their new-found joy.

"It's an answer to prayer," Maggie whispered.

"It certainly is," said Jeff.

Twenty-Seven

The room was bright and warm and the white flannel blanket they had put across Cybil as soon as the baby was delivered felt as if it had just come from the dryer. There was no more pain, and for the moment Cybil had no other thought than to enjoy the rest. Then the baby's cries attracted her attention. A girl, Dr. Barnett had said the instant she was born. Cybil had raised her head and had seen that it was so. A perfect baby girl.

Dr. Barnett handed the baby to a nurse. Cybil's eyes followed the woman around the room as she weighed and measured the baby, then began gently wiping her slick red body clean.

"How are you feeling now, Cybil?" Dr. Barnett asked. When she didn't answer, he looked up from his work. "Caroline," he said to the nurse, "take the baby into the nursery for that."

"No, please," Cybil pleaded.

"It'd be better, Cybil. There's no point in making this more . . ."

"No." The nurse had already wrapped the baby warmly and had her in a plastic rollaway crib. The infant's cries seemed to plead to stay. "Please," Cybil repeated.

"All right." He gestured for the nurse to wheel the crib to Cybil's side. He looked at Cybil and she sensed the forced smile on his lips. She looked back at her baby. She understood Dr. Barnett's concern over her feelings, but she'd have little enough time with the child she'd just borne. She wasn't going to miss a second of what was hers. These few minutes would have to last her a lifetime.

Cybil continued to watch closely as another doctor examined the baby. She'd stopped crying, and the young pediatrician cooed and coddled and sighed sympathetically as he probed her nose and ears with cold steel instruments and shined lights in her eyes. When he was finished he announced a perfectly healthy baby. "I wish they were all like this one," he said, smiling at Cybil. He rewrapped the soft blanket around the tiny, squirming body. "You may hold her now, if you like."

"No," Dr. Barnett protested.

"Please." Cybil looked around the room. Except for the hum of electricity, it was silent. Everyone's eyes were on her. The medicinal smell added to the feeling of distance. The young doctor looked puzzled and waited for Dr. Barnett's answer.

"It's not wise, Cybil."

"For whom, me or your daughter?"

Dr. Barnett looked hurt and tired. He stopped his work and leaned back in his chair. "All right," he said.

The nurse lifted the baby from her crib and settled her in Cybil's arms. Dr. Barnett finished his work, pulled soiled plastic gloves off his hands, dropped them into a wastebasket, and left the room without looking back.

The baby nestled down and turned her searching mouth toward Cybil's body. Cybil ran gentle fingers across the baby's soft cheek, and the baby turned quickly toward her touch. "Oh, you sweet little thing!" Cybil cried. Her eyes flooded with tears, and she wiped at them with a trembling fist. "Take her, please," she said, too quietly to be heard. When no one responded she shouted angrily, "Take her!" A nurse came quickly and took the baby away, and Cybil sobbed.

Jeff felt Maggie squeeze his arm as the huge jet rolled to a stop near the terminal. Maggie's dad would be there to meet them. He had promised that they'd go directly to the hospital. It would be less than an hour before they'd see their new little daughter. The busy terminal was crowded. Jeff carried their bag inside, set it at their feet, and looked over head tops for Dr. Barnett.

"Dad," Maggie called to him once he was sighted.

Dr. Barnett twisted through the crowd. By the time he got to her, Maggie choked with emotion.

"Oh, Dad," she threw her arms around him, stepped back, and wiped her eyes. "It's so good to see you."

Jeff shook his father-in-law's hand.

"How are you doing, little mama?" Dr. Barnett asked.

Maggie giggled, and, as silly as the greeting was, Jeff felt a rush at the sound of it.

"Let's go," Maggie said.

The drive to the hospital was a blur in Jeff's memory. Somehow they'd arrived as if by time warp, appearing in the corridor outside the nursery without conscious thought.

Nursery visiting hours were strictly regulated. It would take some string-pulling by Maggie's dad to get them in to see the baby, even though it would only be through the glass window. Jeff and Maggie waited in the hall as Dr. Barnett went inside to arrange the visit. In a few minutes he reappeared and invited them in.

The curtain behind the viewing window opened as they approached the glass. There were seven babies in little plastic beds within their view. Jeff was surprised there weren't more, until he noted that they were only viewing half or fewer of the infants there. He began searching the nametags attached to the beds for some indication of their baby. He was about to give up in frustration when a nurse wheeled a nursery cart through a far door toward the window where they stood. The smile on her face told them that she had their little girl. Another nurse moved babies around to make room next to the glass.

The baby slept soundly on her back, her fists curled at the top of the blanket that bound her snugly. Her head turned and she made a sucking motion that caused a tiny dimple on her cheek to appear and disappear at regular intervals. She had an ample display of dark hair, but it wasn't nearly the thick shock that Dr. Barnett had described to them. She'd been recently bathed, and a curl had been combed into the damp hair around her face.

Jeff stood beside Maggie with one hand clasped tightly around her waist. Tears gathered in his eyes. He made no attempt to wipe them away until they spilled over onto his cheeks. Then he laughed sheepishly and squeezed Maggie to him more tightly.

"She is beautiful, isn't she?" Maggie said. "I mean, I know every mother thinks her baby is pretty. But this is different. I can be objective . . . in this situation," she added. "She really is beautiful."

Jeff knew she could feel his laughter.

"Well, isn't she?" Maggie looked up at him.

Jeff couldn't answer immediately, and by the time he had control of himself, Maggie had begun to smile at herself as well. "Well, all right, so I can't be objective. So what!"

They spent the evening with Maggie's parents and Gretchen and Carl. They went first to the hospital to show off the baby, then out to dinner when visiting hours were over. And then home again after dinner.

"Carl, she has this little dimple in her cheek," Jeff began as they settled into living room chairs. "The only time you can see it is when she sucks, but she's going to have a knock-out smile."

Carl grinned broadly. "I know. I saw it. Remember, we just came from the hospital."

"What you saw was just a hint of a dimple. Believe me, it's a crater when she's really working at it." Jeff became aware of total silence as he finished talking. He looked around the room. Everyone was staring at him. As he caught their eyes one at a time, they laughed. He blushed and settled back in his chair. "Okay, okay. Laugh. I can take it." And he laughed, too.

Jeff turned out the porch light and locked the front door after seeing Gretchen and Carl to their car. Maggie was already upstairs and in the shower when he came back into the house. He loosened his tie when he heard the shower's flow stop in the adjoining bathroom, and continued to undress, meticulously hanging everything on hangers in the almost empty closet.

He heard Maggie laughing as she came into the room wrapped snugly in a terry bathrobe and drying her curls with a fresh towel. She smelled of shampoo, and her skin was rosy. She smiled again as she drew near to him and he turned to greet her. He sensed that she'd been laughing at him.

"What's so funny?" he asked as she tossed the towel on a chair and reached affectionately around his neck. She kissed him briefly.

"You're funny . . . and cute . . . and sweet . . . and wonderful . . . and . . . " She kissed him again and again with each new compliment.

He liked the activity to every detail except the brevity of the kisses. After the second kiss he put his arms around her back and drew her close to him. He let the game go on for a few more, responding to each one with as much passion as he could manage in the short time she allowed him. Finally he relaxed his hold around her back and took hold of her head, his hands pressing gently at each temple and his fingers touching in the back. He held her for just a moment looking at her face. Then he kissed her, sweetly, letting her go only long enough to embrace her again and bring her close. "I love you," he heard her whisper.

"I love you, too," he said.

Twenty-Eight

Cybil pushed the crochet hook through the swimming edge stitches of the baby shawl she'd nearly finished and picked up a single strand of the pre-cut yarn, pulled a loop through to the back, caught the ends in the hook, and pulled them through the loop. Then she grabbed the blurred ends of the yarn with her fingertips and yanked hard on them, tightening the yarn in place. She repeated the process over and over again. A few more and it would be done, she told herself. She wiped her wet eyes on the sleeve of her robe.

She'd just received a call from the lawyer, Mr. Trenton. He was on his way over with the final relinquishment papers for her signature. Mike had signed his and returned them by mail. That didn't surprise her, of course, but it hurt just the same. She had tried to call Reverend Callahan. The hospital switchboard wouldn't put the call through because it was long distance. The cold, sterile walls of the hospital seemed to close in on her, and she felt like a prisoner. She knew her eyes were puffy and her nose was probably red and shiny. "What do I care?" she said out loud as she reached for a tissue from the box next to her bed.

"What was that?" came a voice from the door.

Cybil looked up to see her lawyer walking toward her.

"Nothing," she said.

"I understand you're going home today."

"Yes."

Mr. Trenton sat in the chair next to her bed and opened his briefcase. He removed a file with her name on it, put it on the table, and relaxed back in his chair. He looked at her intently.

"You've been crying," he said.

"Tactful, aren't we?"

He smiled and looked away for a moment. "I don't believe I can be too blunt at times like these," he said. "I want to know what you're feeling and thinking."

"I feel just great. What did you think?"

"Foolish question." He thought for another moment, then pulled the file into his lap and spoke again. "You don't have to go through with this. The Perrys knew the risks when they got into this thing. They'll get another baby if they don't get yours."

"Are you really that heartless?"

He smiled. "No, I'm not. I feel deeply for you, and you're my client. I know your changing your mind will hurt the Perrys, but . . ." Mr. Trenton opened his briefcase and put the file away. "I won't allow you to sign anything in your present state," he said. "And that's as much to the Perrys' advantage as it is to yours."

"No, wait. I don't want my baby sent to a foster home," she said. "I don't know what I want." The huge knot that grew in her chest rose into her throat. "I don't know what I want!"

"What's this?" a familiar voice asked. Dr. Barnett appeared in the open doorway.

"Cybil's having second thoughts. She's also vulnerable, and I don't think it's a good idea for you to talk to her right now."

"Vulnerable? What are you talking about? I'm her physician, I'm not—"

"You're also Mrs. Perry's father, and . . . "

"It's all right, Mr. Trenton. Dr. Barnett," she began, her heart pounding, "I can't sign those papers right now, but I don't want my baby sent to a foster home, either."

Cybil dried her eyes as Dr. Barnett looked at her thoughtfully.

"I can arrange for the baby to stay in the hospital another day. Perhaps another day to think would help."

"No. I need more time. I want to go home for a while. I'm sorry; I know this will hurt your daughter, but I . . . "

"Yes, it will," he replied, running the fingers of one hand across the furrows of his forehead.

Cybil watched as he leaned forward with both hands resting on the windowsill and stared out of the window, apparently at nothing. His shoulders sagged, and Cybil felt his anguish. She knew she was being selfish, but she also knew that for once in her life her selfishness was justified.

"I wish you'd said something sooner," he finally said. "If only they hadn't seen the baby. It might've been easier." Then he turned back toward her. "Are you going to take the baby with you, then?"

"No! Oh, Dr. Barnett, I don't know what I want to do. Believe me, I didn't want to cause this problem. It's just not as easy as I thought it was going to be. I need more time."

"I think I might have a solution to this." The lawyer tapped the end of his ballpoint in and out with his thumb. "The Perrys have already been approved for adoption, so there's no problem with them taking the baby in the interim. Cybil can make a final decision in a week or two, and —"

"That's great for Cybil and the baby, but what about my daughter? I can't allow her to have that baby for a week or two and then have it taken away from her. It'd kill her."

"Why don't you let her decide that," Mr. Trenton suggested.

Twenty-Nine

Maggie and Jeff's lovemaking of the night before had reaffirmed the legitimacy of their parenthood. That morning, as they dressed and prepared to pick up their new little daughter, Jeff felt closer to Maggie than he had since they'd been married. They had talked until almost morning, and every moment of that private time together had reconfirmed their love for each other.

The day in Norfolk when she'd run away from him, darkness had taken over his life. The light returned when she returned. She had changed since then, or had she? He had been on guard to give her freedom, and she had seemed stronger to him. Perhaps, having not looked before, he hadn't seen her strength. That's what she claimed. The irony was that he felt relieved. A single burden shared by two seemed twice as light.

"Honey! I'd have brought that down," Jeff protested, taking their suitcase from her at the foot of the stairs.

"I know. It's not heavy," she replied. "I'm ready. Let's go."

"It's still early. Your dad said he'd meet us at the hospital at ten." Jeff checked his watch. "Wouldn't you rather wait here?"

"No! I just want to go. Please. Mom, are you coming with us?"

"No. I'll have dinner ready when you get back."

The hospital was no quieter on Sunday morning than it had been on their previous visits. Nurses watched at their stations, doctors roamed the hallways, darting in and out of rooms with clipboards in hand, people lounged in neutral-colored waiting rooms. Jeff waited in line at the cashier's office, and then had to wait several minutes longer while his check was approved. Once that was done, it was just about ten.

The clerk gave him a receipt that identified him and allowed the release of the baby to them. He showed it, as he was instructed, to a nurse at the station near the nursery.

"I'm sorry, Mr. Perry. The baby hasn't been released yet," she said.

"How long will that take?" he asked, wondering at hospital bureaucracy.

"I don't know. There's some problem . . . I, uh, I think you'd better talk to the doctor," she finished as she disappeared behind the nursery door.

"It's all right, Maggie. Just a mix-up. Your dad'll straighten it out when he gets here."

"Where is he?" she cried.

"I'm right here," Dr. Barnett answered from behind them. "Let's go someplace where we can talk," he said, directing them through a door marked Doctors Only. The room was a small lounge, and the three of them took seats in the nearest corner.

"There's no way to soft-pedal this," he began, then paused. "Cybil hasn't signed the relinquishment form," he finally said. "And she's not going to — not right away, anyway."

"No!" Maggie paled and sank back into her chair, turning her face into the corner.

Jeff stood and walked across the room. He folded his arms together above his head and stretched tight muscles. His thoughts bounced off the walls of his brain and became a jumbled mixture — undecipherable. A yellow-edged anatomy chart hung on the wall in front of him, and he stared at it blankly. He turned back to see his wife in her father's arms sobbing uncontrollably.

"Why, Dad?" Jeff asked.

"This is hard for her, too," Dr. Barnett said.

Jeff felt angry. "Don't defend her to us!"

"No. I won't do that. I wish I could change it — make it easier."

"What do we do now?" Maggie asked dully.

"She wants to go home, to Nebraska, I think. She wants two weeks, and —"

"What happens to the baby in the meantime?"

"That's the rough part," Dr. Barnett began. "She'd like you to take her."

"No!" Jeff nearly screamed.

"No," Maggie whispered.

Jeff looked at his wife. Her tears had washed away her makeup. Her face was contorted with pain. She looked pale and vulnerable.

"Maggie." He knelt at her feet and took her hands in his. They were cold.

"Where will the baby go if we don't take her?"

"A foster home, I expect."

"We can't let that happen. This has to work out. Remember, Jeff? It was going to be a sure thing — no more disappointments." Maggie stood and walked to the blank wall across from them. "I guess we have no voice in this, but I want Cybil to take her."

"What?" Dr. Barnett looked lost, and Jeff shrugged helplessly.

Maggie turned suddenly, her tears wiped dry and a new look of determination on her face. "Can you convince her to take the baby home?"

"Yes, I think so. If you don't take her, the foster home is inevitable, and Cybil has already said she doesn't want that."

"But why, Maggie? It'd just increase the risk of losing her."

"In the short run, the risk is greater, but . . . " Maggie turned suddenly. Her chin quivered, making it hard for her to speak. Jeff pulled a handkerchief from his pocket and handed it to her. "Dad, she must be sure of what she wants. We can't take that baby, then lose it again. I want her to be sure."

_____ *Thirty*

"You must be Cybil," Penny said, inviting her into the entry hall. "Rich was pleased to get your call. I'll get him." She walked back through a long hall toward the back of the house.

She's not what I expected, Cybil thought as Penny Callahan greeted her at the front door of the large home. The reverend's wife was dressed in jeans and a flowered T-shirt. Her thick blond hair was tied back with a scarf, and she had a storybook in her hand. Cybil could hear children's voices as the door opened, then closed behind her. In a few seconds the reverend appeared through the same door.

"Cybil." Reverend Callahan walked forward to greet her. "How've you been?"

"I need to talk."

"Of course. I have a little office here that's private, or we can walk down to the church. It's only a couple—"

"Here's fine."

Rich directed her to his tiny office.

"Now. What do you want to talk about?" he asked once they were settled.

Cybil pulled a pack of tissues from her purse and smiled wanly. "I came prepared this time," she said.

Rich smiled back. "I see. I don't wonder that this has been difficult. Begin wherever you like and tell me about it."

"My baby was born two weeks ago, in California. I came home because I can't decide what to do. I'd planned to have the baby adopted out. It was all arranged; I even met the couple. But I couldn't sign the papers." Cybil stopped while she forced the ache in her throat away. "My parents aren't much help," she said. "They want to be, but they aren't. That's why I came here."

"Where's the baby now?"

"With my aunt in California. My parents don't want me to keep her. They don't want to see her."

"The couple you say want to adopt her, are you satisfied they're good people?"

"Yes."

"Then the baby's welfare isn't your worry."

"No. I know what you're getting at . . . it's selfish; I'm being selfish."

"Perhaps, but that's okay. You've had a baby you'd like to love yourself. Giving her to someone else to love is hard."

Reverend Callahan stood and stepped around the desk and sat in a chair across from Cybil. "I'm not sure what you want from me," he said, facing her squarely and taking her hand. "If you want permission to keep your baby in spite of what your parents want, you've got it. That obviously has to be your decision."

"I can't decide. That's the problem."

"What you need is perspective, then." The reverend released her hand and sat back in his chair for a moment. "All right," he said. "I think I can help you with that." He stood again and went to a file cabinet and pulled a picture from one of the folders inside. He handed it to her, then waited.

It was a snapshot of a little boy about a year old. He sat in a high chair, his chubby cheeks pushed back by an engaging grin. His face was smeared with red food stains, and handfuls of red jello oozed out between his fingers. Cybil smiled.

"I've been working at the clinic where I met you since about the time that little boy was conceived."

"He's yours?" Cybil asked.

"No, but I feel almost that close to him. His mother came to me, as you did, at the Women's Health Center. His life was spared that day."

Cybil looked back at the picture and tried to visualize her baby in a year's time. She stepped forward and put the picture on the desk.

"His parents kept him, of course. He brings them joy in every way."

"What are you trying to say? Should I do the same?"

"I can't tell you what to do, Cybil. I'm trying to supply the perspective you wanted." He picked up the picture again and handed it to her.

"Look at it. This time try to picture your daughter in his place."

Behind the child was a fenced-in pool and pool house. Two teenagers played in the yard next to the pool, and a large dog jumped after the frisbee they were tossing. A blurry impression of flowers caught the lower right edge in the foreground.

"I can't give those things to my baby, if that's your point, but I can love her," she said.

"Yes, I know you can."

"Then what do I do? You're confusing me."

"You wanted perspective, and that's what you've gotten." He waited. When she didn't respond, he repeated what she'd said.

"You can't give her *things*, but you can give her *love*. Knowing that the adoptive parents can also give her love, it's up to you to decide whether the things they can give her compensate you for her loss."

"Things are important," she said, thinking of her own childhood.

"Yes, sometimes they are."

"You know, the pool, the dog, even the flowers—they're important."

Her parents had given her things. But her parents had spoiled her; that hadn't been all good. That thought brought into focus an image of Jeff and Maggie Perry standing in the corner of

Mr. Trenton's office discussing quietly an aspect of the adoption they hadn't agreed on. The tear, the gentle touch, the eventual agreement sealed with a kiss. Her eyes flooded with tears. Her daughter's life would be different from what she'd known.

Love and things, love without things—she repeated the words over in her head until they had no meaning. The things would come to her someday, but not without school; and how could she have school with a child to support? Others did it, Reverend Callahan had said a long time ago, but he was talking about couples. She felt that thought tug at her. Mike had signed the papers without a second thought. It wasn't supposed to matter to her, but it did. Mike was out of it—no question. Her head reeled. She could smell the beginnings of the Callahans' dinner, and the blistering Nebraska summer had turned the little office into an oven. She opened the collar of her blouse and wiped perspiration from her face.

"If only I were finished with school, I could make it with a child. But I've barely begun."

"Your parents won't help?"

"Yes, I suppose. Begrudgingly. But even if they did, I'd have classes, and studying, and part-time work. Child care's expensive and risky."

"You've thought this through."

"I've done nothing else for the past two weeks." Cybil's eyes filled with tears. She stood and walked to the only window in the tiny room. It was wide open and overlooked the family's back yard. A fan hummed quietly next to it, and Cybil enjoyed the fresh air it brought into the hot office. "When I took the baby, I told the couple I just wanted to think and be sure. After I got to Aunt Cora's and began really being a mommy, it felt so good, I was sure that's what I wanted. In a way, it's still what I want." She turned back to face him. "My mother called several times that first week. 'The midnight feedings, the diapers, being tied down, babysitters—you'll hate it,' she told me. Reverend Callahan, I've experienced it for two weeks now, and I don't hate it. I know it'll all get tiresome at times, but all those things . . . I love it. That's why it's so hard. If I could put this all on hold— you know, freeze my life the way it has been since the baby was born—it'd work. But I can't. My aunt can't support me, I don't want her to if she could. My parents could, but I don't want that either."

"It sounds like you've decided already." Mr. Callahan put the photo back in its file and closed the cabinet.

"I love my baby!" Cybil cried.

"Of course you do, Cybil." He pulled a handful of tissues from the box on his desk and handed them to her. Then he took her shoulders in his arms and rocked her gently.

"How can I give her up, when I love her so much?"

Cybil carefully shielded the writing paper to keep the tears she shed from staining its surface. The baby slept soundly, and Aunt Cora was out for the evening. Quiet filled the house like porcelain clay poured into a mold. Crickets rasped their noise outside her window, and the smell of gardenias touched her senses. Her chest felt heavy with the task at hand, but she was relieved all the same. The crocheted baby shawl lay folded on the desk in front of her. She absentmindedly fingered its intricate pattern as she thought of what to write. She wondered how many letters she'd have to write before one satisfied her. She had so much she wanted to say, perhaps the tears would say it better.

"I've spent many hours of the past several months," she began.

The baby squirmed in Cybil's arms as she waited on the Perrys' front porch, a small suitcase of baby things and a package resting at her feet. "It's okay, baby," she cooed sweetly. Cybil had stepped from the air-conditioned car to a gust of hot summer air. The Perrys' porch caught a cooling ocean breeze, and she relished the feeling.

"Yes," Jeff said absently as he opened the door, then looked to see who stood there. His eyes widened as he looked first at Cybil, then stared at the infant in her arms. "Come in, please," he said, not daring to believe what he saw. He picked up the parcel and satchel and stepped aside for her.

"Who was that at the—" Maggie came from the bedroom.

"Listen," Cybil began before Maggie could finish.

"This is going to be difficult, so let me speak." She felt a lump build in her throat and stopped until she could swallow it.

"I-uh . . . I'm sorry for the pain I've caused you. It's been hard."
She brushed at her tears with shaky fingers.

"Cybil, we'd—" Maggie reached toward her, but Cybil
backed away.

"No. You don't owe me anything—least of all sympathy. I'm
okay." She stepped toward Maggie and placed her baby in
Maggie's arms. Then she gestured to the baby with a gentle
palms-down motion as if to firmly affix the child's position
there. She stared at her for a long time, then looked at Maggie,
then Jeff. "What can I say? There's nothing more to . . . " Her
words faded and she backed away toward the door.

Maggie's eyes were flooded with tears. She gently clutched
the tiny baby to her body with one arm and futilely wiped at her
face with the other. Jeff stood behind his wife, his full attention
drawn to the child in her arms. They were speechless. *Of course*,
thought Cybil. What was there to say?

Cybil moved closer to the door and Maggie reached toward
her. "Wait. I . . . I don't know what to say. Can't we get you
something? A cold drink, a . . . "

"No. It's best that I leave quickly. I've signed the papers. Mr.
Trenton will have them Monday morning. Oh, here." She
picked up the package and handed it to Jeff. Tears and mascara
stained her face. She bit her lip, then explained, "There's a note."
She opened the front door and left.

The package was all tied up with twine, and Maggie couldn't
break it. She went into the kitchen to look for some scissors. Jeff
held the baby against his chest, her downy head pressed against
his cheek. Tears ran from his face onto the cotton blanket she was
wrapped in. The feeling was unreal to him and he closed his eyes
to make the dream complete. The sound of Maggie plowing
through one drawer after another, searching for the scissors,
ended his reverie, and he enjoyed the reality of his fatherhood
even more.

In a few minutes Maggie came back with a sharp knife. She
laughed and wiped again at the tears that blinded her. "I couldn't
find the scissors. This will do." She put the thin blade under one
section of string and pulled on it until that one popped, then
another. Once the string was off she tore at the paper and peeled
it away from the box. Inside was a large, white hand–crocheted

baby shawl edged all the way around with four-inch-long fringe.

"Oh, it's beautiful," she whispered as she removed it from the box.

"Yes, it is." Tears choked Jeff's words and Maggie looked up at him, and at their baby in his arms.

Maggie found the note and read it to herself. She bit her lip, then pressed trembling fingers against her mouth as if to shield a cry. She handed the card to Jeff, took the baby and wrapped her gently in the beautiful shawl. The fringe tickled the baby's face, and her eyes fluttered. Maggie smiled through her tears and gently pulled the fringe away.

Jeff read the note aloud.

Dear Mr. and Mrs. Perry,

I've spent many hours of the past several months making this shawl for my baby even though I never intended to keep her. I meant to give it to you in the hospital, but when I couldn't sign the papers I couldn't give this up, either. I've signed the papers and mailed them to Mr. Trenton.

All I ask of you is that you love her as much as I do and that you tell her how hard it was for me to give her up. Promise me that, and you'll make this bearable for me.

Sincerely,
Cybil Renwick

Maggie kissed the baby's forehead and pressed her gently to her shoulder. Her head nestled sweetly at the nape of Maggie's neck, and the picture of mother and child touched Jeff deeply. He folded the note and put it back in its envelope.

"I'll write Cybil and tell her we'll treasure her gift. Our baby!" Maggie cried. "She's really going to be ours."

Jeff handed her his already damp handkerchief and she dried her tears. She fingered the shawl's delicate pattern and wrapped the edge of it across the baby's feet. "We'll keep this for our baby. She'll know that her mother . . . she'll know she was loved."